W0018425

Are you a Tiger, a Cat or a Dinosaur?

Are you a Tiger, a Cat or a Dinosaur?

100 Questions: How Competitiveness Influences your Life!

Stephane Garelli

⑤SAGE | Response Business Books

Los Angeles | London | New Delhi
Singapore | Washington DC | Melbourne

This edition is for sale only in South Asia—India, Pakistan, Bangladesh, Nepal, Bhutan, Sri Lanka, Myanmar, Afghanistan and the Maldives.

First published in 2016 by Stephane Garelli

This edition published in 2017 by

SAGE Publications India Pvt Ltd
B1/I-1 Mohan Cooperative Industrial Area
Mathura Road, New Delhi 110 044, India
www.sagepub.in

SAGE Publications Inc
2455 Teller Road
Thousand Oaks, California 91320, USA

SAGE Publications Ltd
1 Oliver's Yard, 55 City Road
London EC1Y 1SP, United Kingdom

SAGE Publications Asia-Pacific Pte Ltd
3 Church Street
#10-04 Samsung Hub
Singapore 049483

Published by Vivek Mehra for SAGE Publications India Pvt Ltd, typeset in 12.5/14 pt Garamond Premier Pro by Diligent Typesetter India Pvt Ltd, Delhi, and printed at Sai Print-o-Pack, New Delhi.

Library of Congress Cataloging-in-Publication Data Available

ISBN: 978-93-864-4620-6 (PB)

SAGE Team: Manisha Mathews, Sunil Koli and Ritu Chopra

To my wife Josephine
whose support made this book possible,
and my son Stephane,
whose help made it better.

TABLE OF CONTENTS

PART III: LEADERSHIP

PREFACE

*A good book is one that raises
a multitude of questions.*

Jean Cocteau

Competitiveness, like social networks, sustainable development or climate change, is a topic that has captured the world. Politicians, businessmen and media constantly refer to it. What does it mean? How does it influence our lives?

For 30 years, I have helped shape competitiveness theory. Yet, the goal of this book is to move beyond academic analysis and illustrate the day-to-day realities of competitiveness.

Today, economic challenges mainly arise from profound changes in society. The priority for companies is less about discovering innovative management techniques and more about offering credible answers to people's and society's new expectations.

What are the most commonly asked questions? This book offers 100. Some deal with competitiveness, while others deal with leadership, society and the world around us. Finally, some are more personal.

There may be several different answers to each of the questions. Therefore, I have made choices. Economics is often a matter of opinion. As John Kenneth Galbraith underscored, economics is "the only science where two people can obtain the Nobel Prize, each saying the exact opposite of each other ..."

So, leaf through the following pages at your own pace, read a chapter where and when you please and take the time to reflect and discover your own ideas.

Finally, I have chosen to write this book using a non-technical style – not something you would expect from a "serious professor." However, I believe that economics need not be complicated or boring to be relevant.

As Paul Valéry once noted:

A serious man has few ideas; a man of ideas is never serious ...

Stephane Garelli, 2017

1

ARE YOU A TIGER, A CAT OR A DINOSAUR?

Competitiveness is not only a matter of strategy and organization. It also increasingly depends on how companies succeed in making two forces cohabit: corporate culture and people's aspirations. With globalization, companies are keen to ensure that employees share the same attitudes the world over. With affluence, a younger generation is adamant about preserving its value system and distinctiveness. This question, and the title of this book, illustrates how competitiveness fares at the intersection of economic constraints, corporate objectives and personal value systems.

A sign of a company's lasting competitiveness is its ability to attract and retain the best talent. In doing so, it needs to adjust to new market realities while recognizing that people's attitudes towards their professional and private lives evolve. Over time, we go through three different stages of motivation:

Tigers: During this stage, we are hungry for success, ambitious and eager to move rapidly up the corporate ladder. Tigers work 60 hours a week or more, are extremely mobile and ready to accept responsibilities anywhere in the world. As their family lives are embryonic – they are neither married nor do they have children – the company is their family and frame of reference. Just like tigers, they have a killer instinct and are capable of being hyperactive and hyper-aggressive in their efforts to succeed.

Cats: After a few years, tigers evolve into cats. The young, up-and-coming executive marries, has children and buys an expensive house with a hefty mortgage. Soon, he will discover the joys of the primary school system through his offspring. His time at work drops to 40 hours a week, more or less. Just like a cat, he remains mobile but wants to be home on the weekends to spend time with his family. His commitment to the company is genuine; however, he is careful to preserve a good work-life balance.

Dinosaurs: After a long life dedicated to the company, the cat turns into another species, a dinosaur. At this stage, life outside the company is more important. Careers have been made and ambitions have been satisfied (or worse, never will be ...). The tiger's killer instinct and the cat's preference for home have vanished; all the dinosaur wants is peace and quiet and to be able to leave the office at 5 p.m. In short, a dinosaur is interested in the balance between his private life and ... his private life (life-life balance). Dinosaurs are not as useless as one might think – they are often the company's living memory, the ones who remember what took place before.

Companies often lose their best executives because they have ignored these changes in attitudes. Promoting a cat to a faraway country will not be happily welcomed because the cat will not want to move his family to another part of the world. Therefore, he will likely refuse such a promotion. In most cases, he will leave the company with the firm belief that no further opportunities will be offered to him and that his loyalty will be questioned.

Global companies are starting to change their attitudes towards work. Some will no longer force senior employees to transfer to a new workplace or a regional headquarters (HQs) for a promotion. They are willing to move work to the executive's country of residence. However, the executive will be required to spend a certain number of days per month at HQs for meetings and informal interactions with senior colleagues. Companies thus adapt to new attitudes, and people to new work standards. Competitiveness thrives on both.

Sometimes my students ask me, "If the ultimate goal is to become a dinosaur, can't we save time and start out by being dinosaurs?" Students are never short of bright ideas. Unfortunately, while tigers often evolve into dinosaurs, the opposite is rarely true ...

PART I: COMPETITIVENESS

A few things that you should know about competitiveness ...

2

ARE YOU AS COMPETITIVE AS USAIN BOLT?

Today everybody talks about world competitiveness; yet, 30 years ago, the term was virtually unknown. If you type "competitiveness" into Google, you will get around 30 million results. However, this new word encompasses a number of different concepts that can be used in many ways. What is competitiveness all about? Usain Bolt can help us understand.

As one of the greatest runners of all time, he is a true example of competitiveness. Why is he so good? Some say it is because he runs fast. However, scientists would qualify this condition as essential but not sufficient.

There are probably hundreds of young men who could run as fast as Usain Bolt, in either Jamaica or elsewhere. However, Usain Bolt was lucky enough to be discovered. He had access to a series of unique facilities: a modern stadium to train in, a good coach, an outstanding diet, an excellent massage therapist and even a sports psychologist to help him improve his mindset. In other words, he became the best because he was able to manage – better than others – a set of resources and competencies.

In the early 19th century, French writer Jean-Baptiste Say defined economics as a science concerned with the production, distribution and consumption of wealth. Over the years, the term "science" has often been replaced by "field of knowledge" and wealth by "prosperity." Within this framework, competitiveness stresses how companies and nations attain their objectives by competing – locally or globally – to gain access to, create and manage the best resources, such as commodities, and the best competencies, such as education.

However, is it taught that way? I remember my university classes in economics where we feverishly learned about interest rates, balance of payments, international trade, supply and demand theory and monopolies. In the real world, it is different. Today, the great questions that affect nations and competitiveness are different. They highlight the importance of sustainability, governance, ethics and education in addition to macroeconomic theory.

Economics and competitiveness have thus increasingly become "holistic," an approach that assumes that the parts of a system are closely interconnected and can only be explained by referencing the whole (*see Question 3: Is competitiveness like playing snooker?*). Moreover, the world economy has become global, which implies that the number of actors and resources available for global competitiveness has increased exponentially.

Nevertheless, the ground rules remain the same. Be it Usain Bolt, Singapore or Google, all have one thing in common: they are at the convergence point of a vast set of resources and competencies that they master better than others.

It means that competitiveness thrives on networking and teamwork. It rewards those who best manage the relationships between the resources and knowledge that they have created or accessed.

In contrast, in the world of competitiveness, those who attempt "to do it all by themselves," in splendid isolation, remain stuck in the losing lane and, indeed, alone.

3

IS COMPETITIVENESS LIKE PLAYING SNOOKER?

Competitiveness is often regarded by many academics as a simple field of knowledge, compared, for example, to financial mathematics or econometrics. This is not completely wrong. Competitiveness, like economics, is fairly straightforward and the basic concepts are easy to grasp. It is not necessary to study for years to realize that inflation is an increase in prices, GDP is a nation's annual income and a trade-balance deficit means we purchase more from abroad than we sell.

But if this is the case, why do we encounter so many difficulties when dealing with economic crises? Why is it so complicated to manage a nation? And why did the Irish playwright George Bernard Shaw once say, "If all the economists were laid end to end, they'd never reached a conclusion."?

The answer is that the basic components of competitiveness are not the issue; the difficulty arises when they begin to interact. The following mental experiment illustrates how it works. Imagine a snooker table. It is rectangular, has six holes and it is lined with a green mat. Snooker is played with a single white ball and 15 colored balls. The first shot consists of shooting the white ball towards the other 15 balls that are assembled in the shape of a triangle. So far, it is easy to conceptualize. Now imagine the first impact, each ball's trajectory and its final position when it stops rolling. The interaction between the balls – simple objects – becomes so complex, has so many parameters and trajectories that it quickly becomes impossible to comprehend how the game will unfold.

The same applies to competitiveness. The relationship between "simple" economic concepts – inflation, debt, budget, trade balance, unemployment, etc. – becomes exceedingly complex when the concepts interact. And this is only the game's first shot. Try to imagine the string of events during an entire game of snooker ... or the succession of economic events during, for example, a recession.

Let us now assume that it would be possible to conceptualize an entire game of snooker. What about replaying it? What if after the first shot an infinite particle of blue chalk remains on the cue? This will be enough to alter the trajectory of the ball and modify the entire game. This is Edward Lorenz's famous "butterfly effect" – a tiny variation in initial conditions can have considerable consequences on the entire system. Chaos theory also describes how such hypersensitivity influences a string of events.

It may also explain our difficulty foreseeing the future. Edward Lorenz was a meteorologist. His science is based on laws that describe immediate events quite accurately, but which have great difficulty anticipating disasters such as cyclones. The same goes for economics.

Ben Bernanke, former chairman of the US Federal Reserve, was a specialist on the 1929 crisis. This helped him during the 2008 financial crisis, but only to a certain extent. Many of the steps he took were unconventional (such as quantitative easing) because the initial conditions of the 2008 crisis were different from those in 1929.

Whether it is playing snooker, forecasting long-term weather conditions or anticipating economic events, the difficulty of managing such systems lies in their sensitivity to initial conditions and the multitude of interactions. How can we learn from the past if the opening rules are reset all the time? Unlike the famously misquoted line from the movie "Casablanca," it is hard to "Play it again Sam!"

4

WHEN WAS ECONOMICS FIRST RECORDED?

Competitiveness thrives on comparing one's performance with those of other nations, companies or individuals. It implies knowing and assessing adequately what you and others are doing and thus recording achievements. In other words, getting the facts first and then analyzing them. This approach is the foundation of the scientific method. However, this has not always been the case for economics.

The emergence of writing in Mesopotamia made it possible to record offerings to temples and commercial transactions. According to Yuval Noah Harari in his book *Sapiens: A Brief History of Humankind*, the first name recorded on a tablet is that of an accountant named "Kushim," not a god or a king, but a record keeper. In Mesopotamia, and later in Egypt and Rome, the economics of a nation consisted mainly of three activities: the allotment of land, the inventory of food stocks and the protection of commercial routes. Wealth was mainly acquired through the spoils of war.

Because wealth was mainly conquered and seldom created, we have few records of it, except for the riches of Alexander's victories in Persia or of Caesars' triumphs over the barbarians. It is said that the first economic treatise is the *Oeconomicus of Xenophon* in 360 BC. From that point and into the 20th century, economists have mostly written their treatises based on philosophy, morality or common sense, with few available facts or statistics to back up their ideas. Gross domestic product (GDP), which is considered the yardstick of economic performance of a nation today, was only invented in the 1930s and first released in the US in 1942 (*see Question 6: Can we trust statistics?*).

What happened in between remained a mystery ... until Angus Maddison, a British economist, and his successors decided to close the gap and calculated the evolution of GDP starting as of year one of our era.

At the time, European countries had a GDP per capita estimated to range between $600 and $800. In 1300, Northern Italy became the richest region with a GDP per capita above $1,600. In 1600, the Netherlands emerged to first place with a GDP exceeding $2,650 per capita. By 1820, it was Great Britain's turn to become the richest nation, thanks to its industrial revolution. For all of them, trading and industry were fundamental to wealth creation.

Some did not take advantage of it as much as they should have. Spain for example, despite its conquests in Latin America and its resources in gold and silver, only saw its GDP increase from $846 per capita in 1500 to $916 in 1800. Its supply of precious metals was not transformed into industrialization. Wealth was acquired but it failed to create it.

The evolution of China is equally thought-provoking. Assuming China had the same GDP as Europe in year one – i.e. $600 per capita – it took a long time to reach that threshold again – 1963 to be precise! This means that for 2,000 years, Chinese leaders failed to increase the wealth of their population. To be fair, Asia, like Africa today, suffered from uncontrolled population growth that curbed the development of individual wealth. Since then, China has caught up, and its GDP per capita is now well over $6,000.

Therefore, throughout history, the fundamental principles of competitiveness were already at work: commerce, industry, transformation of raw materials into products and know-how. Only the ability to systematically record a nation's progress through statistics was missing – until 100 years ago.

5

WHEN WAS WORK RATIONALIZED?

In all likelihood, always ... but at the very least since the existence of spoken language, which made it possible for men to hunt in groups. And later, the arrival of tools paved the way for specialized manufacturing.

During the 12th century, the shipyards in Venice were already able to arm 100 galleons in seven weeks! Standardized production made it possible to have identical parts manufactured and stocked in harbors all around the Mediterranean, which meant vessels could be repaired quickly no matter where they were. In 1571, during the battle of Lepanto, which the Turkish armada lost, more than half of the Christian vessels had been built in the Venetian Arsenal Then, the rationalization of work accelerated in the 19th century with the industrial revolution in Great Britain and the emergence of large factories and companies

The "Liberty Ships" program, which was developed in the United States during World War II, is another great example of rationalization. The US army rapidly needed to transport military equipment for operations in Europe and in the Pacific. To do so, between 1941 and 1945, 2,571 Liberty Ships were built. The first one was named SS Patrick Henry and it was launched on November 27, 1941. It took 225 days to assemble it. The production of the 250,000 parts necessary was rapidly rationalized and specialized. One year later, it only took 70 days to assemble a Liberty Ship. The record was broken by the RS Robert Peary, which was built in 4 days, 15 hours and 26 minutes! The workers' slogan was, "Praise God and move on to another section."

Today, work rationalization continues. After the theorists of the 19th century – American Frederick Taylor (whose scientific management focused on maximizing the productivity of workers) and Frenchman Henri Fayol (whose principles of management focused on the entire organization rather than just the workers) – came the great 20th century thinkers: William Edwards Deming and Joseph Juran for quality processes; Alfred P. Sloan (one of General Motors' most famous presidents) and Peter Drucker (the most renowned management "guru") for work organization in companies.

To a certain extent, globalization and the outsourcing of work to countries with lower labor costs – mostly China and South East Asia – was another aspect of ongoing work rationalization. What is the next stage?

It will probably center on reducing the "human" component in work. Today, there are approximately 1.5 million robots operating in factories the world over. Google is working on a driverless car and driverless trains proliferate. This automation is not only a consequence of technological innovation but also a result of the salary increases in emerging countries (20% to 25% a year); as outsourcing becomes less competitive, automation grows.

Another great disrupter will be the "Internet of Things," whereby machines connected to the Internet will be able to intercommunicate and make decisions. For example, a printer will be able to order ink directly on-line when its reserves are low.

The bottom line is that work rationalization is inevitable and it may even be intimately linked to human nature. Although work will not disappear, it will change; it will be less repetitive, more creative and more intelligent – at least, that is what we hope.

6

CAN WE TRUST STATISTICS?

Benjamin Disraeli's famous remark – "There are three types of lies – lies, damn lies and statistics." – underscores the universal distrust of statistics, especially when they do not conform to our own ideas. In economics, GDP (whether it's growth or decline) continues to be the key statistic that the experts scrutinize. However, we should acknowledge that GDP is an approximate measure of what is really happening. Moreover, it is constantly being corrected.

In recent years, for example, the World Bank has adjusted the Chinese GDP twice – lowering it once and then raising it. Recently Nigeria recalculated its GDP, which gained nearly 89% in one year. Even the prestigious British Office for National Statistics revised its figures: The United Kingdom's GDP experienced a 4.6% leap when it incorporated drug consumption and prostitution into its calculations. Innovation is everywhere!

The US is no better. During the first quarter of 2014, the Bureau of Economic Analysis published a 0.1% increase as its initial estimate for GDP growth. A few weeks later, a revised second estimate showed a decline of 1.0%. The third and final conclusion was a drop of 2.9% in GDP, the worst in years. It was a snowy and unpredictable winter, but still ...

GDP does not calculate the wealth of an economy but the creation of value over a year. It is a comparatively recent invention. It dates back to the interwar period when American President Franklin Delano Roosevelt wanted a more precise idea of the impact of the Great Depression of 1929 on the economy. The American economist Simon Kuznets established the basis of the GDP calculation in the 1930s, and the first publication of the national accounts in this field was in 1942 by the US. Kuznets had a particular way of conceiving GDP because he considered it should only include that which contributed directly to the well-being of society. He excluded advertising, arms and even a great chunk of the financial system from his calculation! Drugs and prostitution were a long way away.

Seventy years later, GDP figures, though scrutinized in an almost religious manner, are still uncertain. Some countries quickly issue their quarterly accounts, such as Singapore and China (within two weeks); others take a little more time, such as the United States and Europe (three to four weeks). Finally, there are countries like Denmark and Switzerland that take their time (more than a month). All proceed to revise their statistics and release their final figures, at best, a year later, which is useless for all concerned. Thus, the question is whether it is preferable to have quick, albeit imperfect statistics, or wait for ones that are more reliable, no matter how late they are.

This is not only a theoretical question. In 2009, for example, the US's statistics did not immediately show the full extent of the financial crisis, and the ensuing recession. Because of this, the Federal Reserve and the Treasury did not react as fast as they could have, had they realized the scale of the problem sooner.

Unfortunately, most economic statistics, such as GDP, only give a blurred representation of reality. Changes to the last decimal do not hold much scientific value.

Economic statistics are like the navigation maps of olden times; everybody knew they were imprecise, but leaders fought hard to lay their hands on them, as there was nothing better. A bad map is more useful than no map at all. The same holds true for statistics; they should be viewed with a critical eye. Then, they can be freely deciphered. As Mark Twain once said, "Get the facts first – then you can distort them at your leisure."

7

DOES ECONOMICS HAVE A MORAL SIDE?

Until the 18th century, the economy basically served to increase the wealth of local rulers – pharaohs, emperors or princes – who stored their valuables in their coffers. Capital was an accumulation of wealth that piled up for the almost exclusive benefit of the leader.

In 1776, when Adam Smith wrote *An Inquiry into the Nature and Causes of the Wealth of Nations*, he emphasized two revolutionary views: The first priority for a state is to increase national prosperity, not the prosperity of the ruler. The second is that capital should not be an end in itself but a means of developing more investments and thus increasing a nation's wealth.

When Adam Smith's book was published, the British industrial revolution was in full swing with technical innovations, such as James Watt's 1769 invention of the steam and piston engine, and entrepreneurs, such as Richard Arkwright, Matthew Bolton and Joseph Wedgwood. Fundamentally, they had the genius to transform technological innovations into enterprises, which would bring added value to raw materials. For example, in 1760, England imported 1,000 tons of raw cotton to feed its textile industry; in 1850, imports reached 222,000 tons!

A new class emerged –the bourgeoisie – that wanted to free itself from the economic yoke imposed by the nobility, which traditionally owned the large estates used for agriculture. It is often overlooked that industrialization requires less use of land since mines and factories concentrate capital and labor in small areas that can be easily bought by upcoming entrepreneurs.

Adam Smith is well known for his concept of the "invisible hand." He believed that individuals who followed their own interests better served the economic interests of all. In the end, they contributed to improving the welfare of nations, as if guided by an invisible hand. In Smith's words, "By pursuing his own interest, he frequently promotes that of society more effectively than when he really intends to promote it."

Though this may appear to justify a "healthy selfishness" in economics, it does not.

In Smith's other great book – *The Theory of Moral Sentiments* – which was written in 1759, 17 years before *The Wealth of Nations*, he argues morality should come first and be the guiding principle of individual behavior. The book offers an insightful reflection on ethics, which must precede and direct our economic actions. It remains relevant 250 years later.

When the middle class gained access to economic and later political power in Europe, it also brought about its own "morality." Contrary to many misconceptions, the industrial revolution that developed in the 19th century was founded on a strict, even ascetic, system of values influenced by protestant and Calvinist ethics. It encouraged such values as work, saving, humility, education, a sense of duty to the community and of assistance to the destitute.

In fact, morality and economics have always been interwoven. Charles Darwin (*see Question 8: Did Darwin defend only the fittest?*) and later Max Weber (*see Question 58: Is austerity a vice or a virtue?*) emphasized this bond with as much strength as Adam Smith did.

We are a long way from the wolves of Wall Street ... A responsible and modern economy should not be as Paul Valéry once said, "A free fox inside an open hen house." Unfortunately, many seem to have forgotten this.

8

DID DARWIN DEFEND ONLY THE FITTEST?

Charles Darwin is mainly remembered for his 1859 book *On the Origin of Species* and his theory that the survival of species depends on their ability to adapt. For many, this idea functions as the foundation for a market economy and competitiveness: only the fittest survive and, by extension, the end justifies the means. Ironically, even Lenin agreed on the latter point.

In his 1871 book, *The Descent of Man*, Darwin reiterates his belief that "there should be open competition between all men, and the ablest should not be prevented by laws or customs from succeeding..." If this is the case, he wondered, where "high moral values" that characterize civilization – such as compassion, pity, assistance to the needy and weak – come from? In theory, these sentiments should never have occurred as they weaken the capacity for survival.

Darwin, therefore, imagines the possibility of group competitiveness (without mentioning this term), not just individual competitiveness. A coherent group without a leader stands a better chance of survival in the long term than a group that is subject to a powerful leader who will eventually disappear and leave the group "orphaned."

From an anthropological point of view, the ability to cooperate within a group is a key factor in the success of the human race. It is also at the heart of competitiveness. Switzerland, for example, is successful because, as a group, it is an *intense* democracy based on a multitude of interactions and counter-powers. The energies reinforce each other.

If we look at France, individuals are highly educated but energies are divided and contradictory. This is what sociologist Emile Durkheim has called "anomie," the disintegration of the moral norms that establish a society.

Northern European countries do not normally seek charismatic leaders because they do not require them. Their societies and successes are based on the cohesion and the intensity of relationships between individuals and social classes. The contradictory debate is not excluded, but it is channeled towards a common objective.

In other countries, social cohesion is replaced by a kind of intellectual discord. It can be brilliant; however, without a well-defined objective, it does not lead anywhere. Such countries often demand "great men" to put order into a system where the individual takes precedence over the group and where social norms have collapsed. The problem is that such great men do not appear every day.

Finally, nations, like groups, survive long term when they have developed a solid aptitude for internal cooperation. Without it, nations weaken or disappear ... Darwin indeed understood that "the" fittest did not apply only to individuals.

9

WHY CARE ABOUT GROWTH?

Obviously, we should care because it increases a nation's prosperity. But what does that mean? And what do people expect from the economy? Some will say growth, but while it's true, it's not enough. Striving solely for growth is like driving aimlessly; eventually, someone will ask, "Where are we going?"

Aurelio Peccei was a wonderful Italian entrepreneur, talkative, cheerful and particularly smart. He created the Club of Rome in 1968. Then in 1972, the Club published *The Limits to Growth*. It is one of the first modern books that asked the question, "Why growth?" It triggered huge debates. Unfortunately, the timing was wrong: A recession started in 1973 and those who had questioned growth were the first to ask for its return!

Economic growth is central to reaching a higher objective: prosperity. How is prosperity defined? In simple terms, it is economic growth plus "something else." This "something else" depends on the state of a country's economic development and value system. In Bangladesh, for example, prosperity is economic growth plus a roof; in Burkina Faso, it is growth plus food; in Mexico, it is growth plus security; in China, it is growth plus consumption and so on. In advanced economies, prosperity could be defined as economic growth plus quality of life and sustainable development.

To illustrate this approach, prosperity can be compared to making a salad. First, you choose the best ingredients: lettuce, tomatoes and carrots. In the case of a nation, these ingredients could be infrastructure, education, administration and technology. Then you need to add the dressing, and you may have noticed that many salad dressings are named after a country – Italian, French, Russian and so on.

Managing a country's prosperity is much the same as making a salad. First, the country competes for the best physical and intellectual resources. Then it's the *dressing* – the value systems that define and bind a population's deeper aspirations – that brings all the ingredients together and differentiates the country. The Chinese, for example, do not have the same expectations for their lives and their nation as their European or Americans counterparts do. Therefore, the competitiveness recipe for each individual country is different, even though the basic ingredients are the same.

Etymologically speaking, the word prosperity stems from the Latin root *sperare* (to hope). Thus, prosperity implies taking into consideration people's aspirations, what they hope to achieve. To achieve this goal, competitiveness provides the economic means, and politics outline the social objectives. Both are interlinked.

The debate on economic growth is often a misleading one. It cannot be isolated from people's aspirations in terms of a better standard of living, education, pension or health care system. There is no prosperity without economic means and there is no competitiveness without politicians giving a sense of purpose to a nation's effort. A nation that does not enjoy economic growth is a nation that must reduce people's expectations, which happens during recessions.

If competitiveness is the tool, prosperity is the objective. Successful nations generally have a strong consensus on what should be achieved collectively. They have a blueprint for economic growth and prosperity. Others drift from one crisis to another.

As Seneca pointed out, "If one does not know to which port one is sailing, no wind is favorable."

10

WHAT SHAPE WILL THE NEW ECONOMIC CYCLES TAKE?

When he became Prime Minister of France, Raymond Barre was introduced by President Valéry Giscard d'Estaing as the best economist in the country. It was true. Generations of students had learned economics from the manuals written by Barre, who described himself as a square mind in a round body. He once told me, "Garelli, economy is only a matter of cycles; the problem is, we don't know when they start, how long they will last and when they will finish ..." At the time, I was not especially impressed ... yet ...

It is normal for an economy to accelerate or slow down depending on the domestic or international economic climate. According to today's definition, a recession is a reduction in GDP for two consecutive quarters. However, the duration of a recession is more important than knowing whether or not one exists.

Some recessions take the shape of a V – deep but short – and these mainly take place in the US. Others are trickier; they start as a V and then the cycle repeats itself, thus resulting in the shape of a W. This happened after the 2008 crisis in countries such as Italy. There are also U-shaped recessions, which last longer and occur mostly in Europe. Finally, there are the L-shaped recessions, where growth collapses and remains flat for a long time; it used to be a specialty of Japan, but now it is spreading.

With the 2008 crisis behind us, it is likely that we will see a change in the economic cycles of advanced economies. It is possible that the traditional economic paradigm of perpetual growth that is only interrupted by short periods of recession will be reversed; instead, long periods of "soft growth" will be interrupted by short periods of fast growth. During the periods of soft growth, the economy may experience either stagnation or deflation, or both.

To illustrate this, we could compare the economic cycles prior to 2008 to a cyclist riding at full speed who falls from time to time, gets up and resumes his race. The post-2008 economic cycles would be more like a donkey ride – a gentle pace interrupted from time to time by unanticipated short bursts of activity that no one understands. In these new post-2008 cycles, the rules of the game for companies are obviously cost efficiency and resilience. They demand that companies have a capacity to bounce back rapidly during active growth periods to take advantage of them.

In the end, the worst legacy of a period of economic slowdown is when it turns into a mindset. Companies permanently reduce costs and freeze salaries. Consumers become cautious, even anxious and postpone purchasing non-essential goods. In other words, everybody waits and nothing happens.

Only financial markets maintain some activity but they are increasingly unpredictable. Finance alone cannot be a substitute for economic activity. If the real economy experiences cycles, finance cannot escape the consequences.

As John Maynard Keynes said, "Markets can remain volatile longer than you can stay solvent!"

11

DO WE NEED THE RICH?

To pay taxes? This is indeed what some politicians believe: Their talent for creating new taxes knows no bounds! In fact, taxes are often a necessity; eleven governments in Europe currently spend over 50% of their GDP. Discussing wealth today also implies addressing the issue of inequality. The Oxfam foundation estimates that global wealth amounted to $241 trillion in 2013. It reveals that 1% of the world's population enjoyed $110 trillion whereas the other 99% (7 billion people) shared the remaining $131 trillion.

According to the stereotype, the wealthy are often viewed as idle, useless and disconnected from reality. That may have been true in the past, i.e. before and immediately after the industrial revolution as many were living off their capital. It is less true nowadays. In a modern society, many young people aim to become rich through their work. It is an essential driving force in society.

The younger generation needs hope – the hope to become as successful as Thomas Edison or Bill Gates. Why work hard and take risks if, ultimately, it means earning the same income as someone who watches TV all day?

Equal opportunities at the start of one's life (one of the missions of education) shouldn't be confused with equal results at the end. Every modern society must accept a latent inequality that rewards effort, from which everyone benefits. The debate on wealth distribution stresses that the accumulation of capital should not lead to a closed, egotistical class, which creates nepotism and excludes newcomers, as was the case for the nobility of the past.

Joseph Schumpeter summed it up: The wealthy class in a society should be like "hotels that are certainly always full, but whose clientele changes constantly ..." Previously, Alexis de Tocqueville had a similar idea: "The wealthy emerge daily from the masses, to which they endlessly return ..." This was the basis for his famous equal opportunity theory that favors social mobility.

This principle is best illustrated in the United States: The Rockefeller, Vanderbilt or Morgan families, which made their mark in the early 20th century, have nearly all vanished. Wealth bears new names: Bill Gates, Sergey Brin, Steve Wozniak, Paul Allen, Jerry Yang, Warren Buffet and Larry Ellison. Capital continues to be generated, but its ownership changes regularly.

A modern economic society must favor the "social ladder." The greatest risk of an extreme concentration of wealth is that it limits advancement from one class to the next. Until now, the system has worked relatively well. Dynasties of wealth disappear regularly to the benefit of new entrepreneurs, according to Joseph Schumpeter's principle of "destructive creation."

Nevertheless, politicians, particularly in a democracy, find it increasingly difficult to deliver a credible message regarding wealth and its accumulation. Is it the natural reward for entrepreneurial success in a dynamic and open society? What is *natural*? Alternatively, are we drifting towards a plutocracy?

As Winston Churchill said: "The inherent vice of capitalism is the unequal sharing of blessings; the inherent virtue of socialism is the equal sharing of miseries." Is there a middle road?

12

CAN YOU BE RICH AND USELESS?

Yes, and it does not require a lot of effort! For instance, if you inherit a sizable fortune, you can spend most of your life lying on a sunny beach in the Caribbean. While your body and mind go soft, you can experience the sweet sensation of being rich ... and the utter uselessness of doing nothing. Meanwhile, your fortune will also melt away because an inheritance that is not actively managed disappears. That is what generations of wealthy families have experienced in the past; today, they are an almost extinct species.

The same holds true for nations. Wealth, lifestyle or even political power do not equate to competitiveness. There are in fact two sources of inherited wealth for a nation.

The first is obtained from the exploitation of natural resources. The most striking example is the discovery of oil and natural gas in Saudi Arabia. In one generation, a barren land became one of the richest in the world. This works well for the people in countries with a small population. The benefits are less obvious for larger states. Brazil, Russia, Nigeria, South Africa and India are all potentially rich countries in terms of natural resources. However, their populations do not benefit in the same way that countries with smaller populations do.

The second source of inherited wealth is derived from the competitiveness of our forebears; it is inherited. Great Britain and France are wealthy countries because they have benefitted from industrial and colonial empires created by previous generations. Do they remain competitive today? That is another story ... Simply put, a generation's wealth is often the consequence of the competitiveness of its parents.

Why do countries that are rich in natural resources remain uncompetitive? Is there a "curse" on countries with raw materials? Great Britain had raw materials such as coal and iron in the 18th century. However, instead of exploiting and exporting them, Britain transformed them into finished products such as steel, machines and ships or used them to run textile and china factories, for example. This transformation process towards creating added value, characterized the industrial revolution, and it is the foundation of competitiveness.

Dubai is a recent example of this principle. I visited the Emirate for the first time in 1978, seven years after the independence of the United Arab Emirates. It took several hours to drive from Abu Dhabi to Dubai, dodging camels and waiting for the car to cool off. Contrary to its rich neighbor Abu Dhabi, Dubai's oil reserves were running out quickly.

Beginning in 1995, Sheikh Mohammed Bin Rashid Al Maktoum, in his role as Crown Prince, and later as leader of Dubai, started a diversification policy that included tourism, transportation, logistics, data processing, banking and media all of which are responsible for the success we see today. If Dubai's oil reserves had not been declining, perhaps the Emirate would never have become competitive.

Similar to Dubai, the most competitive countries for a long time have been without any, or only a few, raw materials. Japan, Switzerland, Singapore and Denmark are some examples. These countries have had to diversify, transform and re-export in order to survive. It was the only recipe for success. They did not have a choice; they did it or they disappeared economically. Some call it a blessing in disguise.

13

IS BORING COMPETITIVE?

"It's amazing! I was sure the Swiss were boring!" I never tire of this compliment that I sometimes receive after a keynote address abroad. I apologize profusely and promise to be dull the next time. Why are the Swiss stuck with this reputation? True, we are not known for our lightheartedness or for being the life and soul of a party. Swiss humor is not considered subtle. Some say it is because we are serious ... seriously boring.

Yet this austere side is part of our competitiveness. The Calvinism that has molded the history of Switzerland compels people to live in utmost discretion. In Switzerland, wealth whispers and success is unassuming. All of these qualities are perfectly adapted to the core industries of banks and insurance companies that sustain Swiss competitiveness.

Personally, I prefer my bank to be boring. In fact, I tend to worry when it offers exotic products. Moreover, as far as my insurance is concerned, I am not sure that a pronounced taste for complex new services reassures me. In short, boredom – sorry, seriousness – is a comfort to me.

It is true that the competitiveness of a nation or enterprise is the result of its ability to innovate. Boring Switzerland performs rather well in this regard. It regularly figures among the top nations in the index for global innovation of the World Intellectual Property Organization (WIPO), and in the number of Nobel prize-winners per capita in science. Switzerland also has one of the highest numbers of patents per inhabitant. In addition, the Swiss have an uncanny ability to transform innovations into products. In fact, 90% of competitiveness lies in the excellence of execution.

Until recently, this manufacturing acumen has contributed to the success of Japan, most of South East Asia and, of course, China. For example, Japan and Korea top Asia for the number of patents in force: in 2013, Japan had 2,001 patents per 100,000 capita, and Korea had

1,507. But these are not patents for new products; they are often patents that apply to improvements in task execution. Tablets, mobile phones and modern genetics were invented elsewhere.

In life, there are situations where it is vital to be boring. For example, when you are comfortably seated in a plane before take-off, you might reflect, "Let's hope the pilot does not want to show us his aerobatic manoeuvers." The same applies to trains: we want them to be on time and to follow the same route. Boring is reassuring and efficient.

Ninety percent of competitiveness depends on delivering what is expected. Not everybody is an inventor like Thomas Edison or Bill Gates. Although it is less exciting, but being boring (or serious ...) often has the surprising effect of comforting clients.

So if this is the price of success, a boring business model may not be that bad.

14

IS "SOCIETAL CAPITALISM" THE FUTURE?

Flashback: On October 24, 1907, at 1:30 p.m. a very agitated man arrived at 23 Wall Street, the offices of the famous financier J.P. Morgan. The caller was the President of the New York Stock Exchange, Ransom "Pay Me" Thomas. He was invited in. He got straight to the point: If he didn't have $25 million by 2:30 p.m., 50 brokers would go bankrupt and the stock exchange would close.

J.P. Morgan acted fast. He immediately summoned 14 presidents of large banks and gave them 10 minutes to raise the funds. At 2:16, they had already assembled $23 million. A few minutes later, J.P. Morgan heard thunderous applause from the stock exchange across the street. The financial system was saved.

September 15, 2008. The world is in shock – Lehman Brothers is bankrupt. Continuous loops on television showed employees in tears and emptying their desks. A few days later, the insurance company AIG was on the brink of insolvency. This time, however, there was no J.P. Morgan to save the financial system. Where were the bankers? They were nowhere to be found. The motto quickly became "Every man for himself and the government for all ..." This abdication of responsibility was dramatic. This was the moment the economy changed forever.

Governments stepped in to take control of the economy. It turned into a settling of scores: new taxes and especially new legislation. In the financial sector, the Basel III regulations outlined by the Bank for International Settlements contained some 616 pages. The Dodd-Frank Act in the US had more than 840 pages while the enforcement rules exceed 20,000 pages. A new state-backed capitalism was born, not just in advanced economies. In China, Russia and the Gulf countries, this kind of capitalism was flourishing. In addition, all states increased their hold on the economy through sovereign funds that today manage more than $7 trillion.

However, this new capitalism will not be enough to prevent other crises. At the root of the problem is what economists call "the asymmetry of information," a theory for which Joseph Stiglitz, Michael Spence and George Akerlof received a Nobel prize in 2001. To make it simple, some people have access to information that others do not have (in 1815, Nathan Rothschild knew the outcome of the battle of Waterloo before the London Stock Exchange thanks to carrier pigeons). Others – and this is new – understand information that others do not (for example complex financial products).

And this problem of imperfect information about markets is here to stay; whether it is state-backed or private capitalism, rules will always be written and implemented more slowly than problems arise.

The only way to avoid excesses and unacceptable practices is for companies to define and implement new ethical standards themselves, albeit sometimes under the pressure of public opinion. Globalization should not mean becoming insensitive to the concerns of the community in which one operates. Good governance, transparency and ethics are necessary.

The debate between "privately owned" and "state-backed" capitalism is indeed relevant. However, a new civil society has emerged. It is global, informed and interconnected. It believes that a business's responsibility should extend beyond profitability and stakeholder interests. It advocates that companies should start to address issues affecting society, even though they do not directly affect their activities and they are not imposed by law.

In short, society calls for a new "societal capitalism." But when?

PART II: THE WORLD

Competitiveness existed before; now it is everywhere ...

15

WHAT ARE THE ROADS TO PROSPERITY?

Fernand Braudel is one of the greatest historians of the 20th century. In his book *The Mediterranean and the Mediterranean World in the Age of Philip II*, he emphasized a new approach to history: "La longue durée" (the long-term perspective). One, day he ironically swept aside the argument of a critic with this snappy reply, "After all this is merely an event." What about economics? (His other major work is *Capitalism and Material Life*.) Are there some constants that go beyond the eventful and endure through the ages?

Actually, there are – commercial routes. Whether by land or by sea, the attempt to dominate commercial routes has been a constant in history. Over the ages, they have defined the struggle among empires, nations and corporations. In a way, this is where the race for competitiveness started. The ambition to control the great trade routes and reap their economic benefits can usually explain the great political events that have influenced the history of the world.

The Bronze Age relied on the copper and tin routes from the Northern Steppes to produce this new alloy. Then came the iron road from Anatolia where the Hittites had mastered iron's production. The wheat route started on the shores of *Euxinos Pontos* (the Black Sea), and it was mainly controlled by the Phoenicians and the Greeks in the Mediterranean Sea. Later came the frankincense and myrrh route that originated in Yemen; these incenses were used in palaces, temples and churches. One of the longest, and perhaps the most famous, remains the Silk Road, which linked Xi'an in China to Rome. In modern times, history was fashioned by the gold and silver routes from the New World and the spice route from faraway islands in Maluku or the Indian Ocean. And let us not forget the most appalling route of all: slavery.

In 1803, when Napoleon sold Louisiana to President Jefferson for $15 million, neither had exact knowledge of the particulars of the territory, which stretches from the Gulf of Mexico to the 50th parallel. (Today we know that it represents 2,144,000 km^2 or four times the size of France; thus, it doubled the size of the United States at the time). President Jefferson commissioned Meriwether Lewis and William Clark to explore this new land and find a navigable route to open trade towards the Pacific. The Ohio, Mississippi, Missouri and Columbia rivers soon became the main routes to American prosperity.

And it goes on. China has embarked on the development of a huge trade route through Central Asia, the "Silk Road Economic Belt." It will be supplemented by the expansion of maritime shipping routes through the Indian Ocean and the Persian Gulf, the "Maritime Silk Road." China can already boast seven of the ten largest commercial ports in the world.

Will traditional routes survive the emergence of the new electronic routes and e-commerce? Electronic routes can replace traditional ones when the product can be dematerialized, e.g. information, books, music and images. However, in most cases, these routes will complement each other rather than compete with each other. The majority of goods ordered electronically still need to be shipped and delivered. Amazon, the largest online store in the world, continues to depend on commercial routes to serve its clients; and if someday drones deliver the goods, air traffic lanes will likely be secured.

Oddly enough, whether old or new, tangible or dematerialized, routes seem to share and attract the same uninvited troublemakers: pirates and hackers! It underlines another historical constant: routes are only valuable and competitive as long as they are secure ...

16

HAVE WOMEN BEEN VICTIMS OF THE PLOW?

Gender inequality remains one of the most contentious forms of inequity in the world. It does not stop there. There is inequality within inequality. For example, the United Nations Development Program reveals that Northern European countries like Holland, Sweden, Denmark and Finland have a greater tendency to include women in society than Colombia, South Africa, Venezuela, Jordan, Indonesia, Qatar or India. Why?

In the history of the world, gender discrimination has not always been the rule. From the prehistoric era to the early civilization in Mesopotamia, and later in the Cyclades, people have adored omnipotent goddesses, symbols of the nurturing Earth or fertility. Numerous societies have developed based on the all-powerful matriarchy. Then something changed ...

The French historian Fernand Braudel believes it happened during the 5th millennium before our era, probably in Mesopotamia, with the invention of the plow. Masculine strength became necessary to handle the plow; thus, women were replaced in the fields ... and in society.

How is it that 7,000 years later, we are still hostages to this technological innovation? Researchers Alberto Alesina, Nathan Nunn (Harvard University) and Paola Giulano (UCLA Anderson School of Management) have discovered that in countries where agriculture is dominated by the use of the hoe, such as Rwanda, Botswana, Madagascar or Kenya, women are more involved in work. In Burundi, 91% of women work outside the home. In other countries, where agriculture was based on the plow, like India or Egypt, women stayed at home.

Some theories hypothesize that climate change may also have induced people to move away from a foraging culture and develop intensive farming. The advantage is that crops with a shorter yield such as wheat, barley or rye increase food supply and security. On the other hand, they necessitate the use of tools and especially the plow.

But are today's societies, where the plow has been replaced by the tractor, still influenced? Indeed, the deep social structure of a country is often rooted in its past agricultural culture, even long after the agricultural culture has disappeared.

One of the interesting aspects of microcredit is that it places women – or, rather, groups of women – at the center of the system and makes them collectively responsible for the loan. Whether in Bangladesh, India, Latin America or, more recently, Africa, the observation is the same: When men obtain loans, they tend to spend them on drink or buy weapons. Women generally invest the money in entrepreneurial activities and pay back the loan.

Elsewhere, disparities remain. In so-called developed countries, women represent between 45% and 50% of the working population. However, the "glass ceiling" remains. In business, particularly in large companies, the situation is evolving; today, a woman can manage General Motors or Yahoo.

In politics, it is a different story. It is true that in Sweden, women occupy 44% of the seats in parliament, ahead of Finland. But the proportion in the US is only 17%, in Japan 13%, in Russia 11% and only 9% in Brazil. The plow still looms …

17

IS THE WORLD
BECOMING LESS POOR?

In times of recession, the market economy is accused of being the source of all evil. In some cases, the allegation is justified: fabulous bonuses, golden parachutes, a lack of transparency, questionable ethical conduct, etc. The market economy, nonetheless, is a highly adaptable and efficient instrument for the creation of prosperity.

Never before has so much wealth been created as it has during the past few decades. Thirty years ago, the United Nations Development Program proposed that rich countries devote on average 0.8% of their GDP in development aid to poor countries. The target was never reached. Economic growth is driven by companies, not bureaucrats.

It is precisely by implementing the principles of a market economy that emerging markets have attained unprecedented growth. In 1995, China's GDP was approximately $700 billion. By 2015, it had increased 15-fold! Soon, China will become the world's largest economy.

In 1981, 52% of the world's population lived below the poverty line, defined by the World Bank as $1.90 (purchasing power parity adjusted) per day. By 2012, the percentage had dropped to only 12.7%! However, not everybody has benefitted to the same extent: 48% of the African population is still poor, compared with only 12% in China. In all, nearly 2.8 billion people are reaching the early stages of prosperity, which has created not only an economic but also a human transformation. If the world is less poor today, it is thanks to the growth generated by the market economy, rather than any grand international program.

The power of the market economy and its capacity to create growth stems from the fact that it is capable of reinventing itself. In contrast, planned economies have collapsed because they were unable to accept internal criticism – a logical outcome for systems that believe they are based on absolute truths, so they will not change.

In his book *The Open Society and its Enemies*, the Philosopher Karl Popper stressed that the real superiority of democracies is that they are able to withstand criticism. As long as a system can openly confront its internal dissensions, it becomes stronger, reforms itself and survives. The day it no longer has this ability, it disappears. The same goes for the market economy.

Of course, exuberant growth creates its own problems – pollution, global warming, urban migration, social inequalities. The realization came in 1972 when Aurelio Peccei, the founder of the Club of Rome, sounded the alarm and challenged the benefits of uncontrolled growth. Then in 1987, Gro Harlem Brundtland, the Prime Minister of Norway for several terms, initiated the concept of sustainable development in a report to the United Nations entitled *Our Common Future*.

Al Gore, with his book and movie – *An Inconvenient Truth* – extended the debate in public. Finally, there was the Paris Climate Conference – COP21 – in December 2015, where 195 countries adopted the first ever universal climate deal. The agreement is supervised by the UN and it will enter into force when at least 55 countries representing 55% of global emissions deposit their instruments of ratification.

However, if the world has become less poor today, it is mainly because more and more countries have been inspired by the principles of the market economy. It has been so successful precisely because it is able to continually reform itself and face criticism.

In economics, there are no absolute truths ... but there may be some realities.

18

WHERE DO OUR PRODUCTS COME FROM?

In a globalized economy, it is becoming harder to tell. A few years ago, researchers at the University of California traced the origins of the 431 components of an iPod. They came from all over the world to be assembled in Longhua, China, in the Foxconn factory. Surprisingly, China's added value to the product did not exceed 3% of the total. However, upon arrival at the US customs, the iPod was statistically counted as a Chinese import. So is Apple Chinese?

Apple's iPads are more explicit. They are labeled, "Designed in California, assembled in China." Why do we need to know where a product comes from? Essentially for tax reasons (for example, customs duty rates differ in the European Union depending on whether or not a product is labeled European), or for compensation reasons if a product is subject to anti-dumping tariffs (for example, Chinese solar panels). However, what happens if a product is assembled from multiple components?

A few years ago, the GATT's Multifibre Arrangements imposed export quotas by country. Chinese cashmere exporters, who had exhausted their quota for sweaters, had the idea of shipping sweaters to Indonesia (which had a reserve of unused quotas) and having a "Made in Indonesia" label sewn on them. Then everything was shipped to Europe as an Indonesian product. Today the Kyoto Convention (in effect since 1974) sets norms for the origin of products either according to the percentage of local content (above 50% or 60%) or according to the principle of the last and most important transformation process (which had to be more than sewing on a label).

Look at the origin of the products you have at home. For example, there are more than 100 domestic appliances. Of course, most come from Asia, and even if some brands look "homegrown," they have likely been manufactured in Asia. Today 90% of the toys sold in the

United States come from China (particularly from Shenzhen). Barbie, for example, is more Chinese than meets the eye ...

So, where can you find local products? In your medicine cabinet or your fridge, but not necessarily! The globalization of our food supply – from Brazilian mangoes to Vietnamese shrimps – is just as impressive and nearly as pervasive as the components in our tablets ...

Is there any harm in this? Not necessarily because the globalization of products has allowed poor countries to develop. It has also given Europe and the US access to cheaper products (*see Question 63: Is inflation addictive?*). Besides the impact on jobs, there is also the issue of identity: A country is intimately linked to what it makes. In public opinion, Switzerland means watches, Italy clothing and the United States, electronics. And Great Britain? Well, there it is a bit harder to tell ...

The "Made in" concept is again becoming a major issue (*see Question 19: Should we care about "Made in?*). The "re-industrialization" of advanced economies is back in fashion. Consumers are more and more sensitive to the local aspect of a product, whether it's food or craftsmanship.

Identifying where a product comes from is often a key aspect of its attractiveness. Back to the future ...

19

SHOULD WE CARE
ABOUT "MADE IN"?

A country's image and reputation are intimately linked to what its companies produce. The emergence of Japan as an economic power is often associated with the arrival of Sony transistor radios or Toyota compact cars in our markets. Germany's image of competitiveness was also built on brands such as Mercedes, BMW, Audi, Siemens, Bayer – all excellent manufacturers. France is known for its luxury (LVMH) and the US for its technology (Apple, Google, HP and many more). And, today Great Britain is identified with ... not much, actually.

All the mythical names of British industrial success – from Rolls-Royce to Cadbury – have disappeared or they have been bought out by foreign companies. Of course, a few companies such as GlaxoSmithKline (GSK) in pharmaceuticals remain.

Great Britain, home of the industrial revolution, has de-industrialized through the decades. In 1950, the manufacturing industry represented 39% of the country's added value; today it has dropped to 12%. Services now represent around 70% of its GDP and industry accounts for only 25%. When *Forbes* magazine ranked the ten largest British companies before the 2008 crisis, six were financial institutions. The same trend can be observed in the US: 16% of profits came from the financial sector in 1980; by 2008, this figure had risen to 41%!

Therefore, the "Made in" label that indicates a product's origin is not without significance. Eventually, the consumer eats or uses a tangible product. Economically powerful companies or nations "make" things that consumers can recognize and identify with. Nowadays, China manufactures more than 20% of the world's products, i.e. as much as the US. Abroad, I am sometimes told, "Switzerland is banks and insurance companies ..." Yes, of course, but it is also watches, food, pharmaceuticals, specialty chemicals, precision mechanics and consumer electronics; in short, manufacturing. The same goes for Germany, where manufacturing represented almost 21% of the GDP in 2015.

Should some outsourced production in emerging economies be repatriated? That's what many CEOs think: General Electric in the US has brought part of its domestic appliances division back to Louisville, Kentucky from China. The American Council for Competitiveness estimates that 3 million jobs could be created in the US if more enterprises decided to repatriate their production facilities.

This concept is called "reshoring." The problem is that jobs created on the way back are not the same as those lost on the way out. New factories in Europe and the United States are highly automated and robot-intensive. Consequently, jobs associated with their operation are increasingly white collar engineering jobs rather than blue collar manufacturing jobs.

A country's capacity to produce is at the heart of its competitiveness, and countries that have succeeded such as Germany, Sweden and Switzerland have all been able to preserve their industries. However, in these countries, the nature of manufacturing is probably changing. It will concentrate on innovative technologies and products with higher value-added or hallmark brands.

Even if services are dominant in a modern economy, a country's prosperity will continue to depend on maintaining and developing sophisticated manufacturing capacities. As Charles Dickens once said, "Industry is the soul of business ...." It still holds true today ...

20

CAN CHINA INVENT?

Indeed, China can! It would probably be easier to identify what China did not invent, than the contrary. In 1954, the British researcher Joseph Needham published an encyclopedia entitled *Science and Civilization in China* in which he listed the main innovations developed in ancient China. The list is impressive: the plow, cast iron, the compass, steel, the parachute, the crank, the suspension bridge, the wheelbarrow, the rudder, lock-gates, the loom and, of course, paper money, gunpowder, etc. All of these inventions and many others were made in China long before they were "reinvented" in Europe a few centuries later.

Everybody knows that Christopher Columbus "discovered" America in 1492. He headed an expedition of three ships, each approximately 22 meters long. It has only recently been discovered, that in 1421 a fleet led by the Chinese admiral Zheng He had crisscrossed the different oceans of the planet and in particular the fleet had been to America. His fleet counted more than 100 ships, some 160 meters long. Of course, Christopher Columbus was unaware of this ...

What is surprising is that upon Zheng Ho's return to China, all traces of his expedition were erased. Similarly, under the Tang dynasty (618 to 907 A.D.), China had become an extraordinary technological power ... yet these innovations were not transformed into an industrial revolution.

Today China is again enjoying not only economic growth, but it also has a capacity for invention. It is visible in industries such as solar panels, batteries, communications, etc. Today, there are more than 3 million active researchers in China, approximately eight times more than in France.

Too often, it is believed that the development of East Asia has been based on a capacity to copy Western inventions and manufacture them more cheaply and quickly. At the start, this may have been due to the economic strategy of Japan. Sometimes I ask my students to mention one fundamental invention made by Japan since World War II that has changed our lives, and the Walkman does not count ...

After moments of puzzlement, and a few guesses such as television, video or computers, my students face the facts: the competitiveness of Japan was mostly based on the rapid transformation of Western inventions into cheaper yet good-quality products. Nonetheless, Japan is a nation that holds an impressive number of patents. For the most part, they are application patents, not inventions. Today, things are changing as demonstrated by the 2014 Nobel Prize that was awarded to three Japanese researchers (at the universities of Nagoya and California Santa Barbara) for their work on efficient blue light-emitting diodes (LED).

China, on the other hand, will quickly renew its long tradition of fundamental research. The competitiveness of its companies won't solely be based on low prices, but also on innovative technologies and endogenous inventions.

It will be highly stimulating for everybody. Indeed, Chinese scientific thinking is not as dependent on the methodology of Descartes or Newton. It is often more "holistic." In contrast to a more specialized Western approach, it favors bridges between different domains of knowledge. This diversity of viewpoints also explains the extraordinary contribution to modern science of the other great intellectual power in Asia: India. Now it is China's turn.

21

ARE LOW WAGES NECESSARY
TO BE COMPETITIVE?

There are few questions in economics that are as debated and emotional as this one. On the one hand, there are those who argue that low wages make it possible to control costs, guarantee the future of enterprises and preserve jobs. On the other hand, there are those who argue that higher wages increase purchasing power, which in turn increases the demand for companies' products and makes it possible to sustain employment (this was, in fact, Henry Ford's approach. He decided to "overpay" his workers, so that they would be able to purchase the cars he produced). The answer to this question is, "It depends ..."

Today, the highest wages (total compensation in manufacturing in 2014) are earned in Denmark, Norway and Switzerland: Over $40 an hour. Germany is around $33, the United States is at $25, China is at $3.5 and India is less than $1. Surprisingly, the most competitive countries in the world are situated all over this scale. In the IMD report on nations' competitiveness, the US is regularly first, Switzerland second and Germany and Norway are always among the top 10. China is 21st and India is 40th! Thus, it is not easy to find a direct correlation between the cost of labor and competitiveness.

"It depends" because the cost of labor cannot be considered in isolation from other factors. The first is productivity: High labor costs can be justified if, in turn, productivity is equally high. In the ranking for labor productivity (GDP per person employed, per hour and per dollar), we find among the first 10 countries Norway, the US, Denmark and Switzerland (more than $50 and very competitive) whereas China is 56th ($8) and India 60th ($5).

The second factor is the positioning of enterprises. If Switzerland is competitive in spite of high labor costs, it is because companies have concentrated on premium brands (for example, the luxury and watch industries) or on industries with higher added value (such as precision mechanics and pharmaceuticals). Companies would find it hard to be competitive in Switzerland with a low-price strategy. However, the opposite is true in India where the advantage conferred by low wages can be exploited by enterprises in domains such as data processing or call centers, e.g. the Bangalore region.

Whatever the positioning of its enterprises, a nation must remain focused on the overall evolution of its salaries in relation to productivity. Twenty years ago, salaries in Ireland were approximately half of those in Great Britain, only an hour's plane journey away ... Today, and despite the crisis, Irish salaries are on average 15% higher than those in Great Britain ($29 vs. $25). Fifteen years ago, salaries in Hungary were 13 times lower than they were in Germany. Nowadays, they are only five times lower ($6 in Hungary vs. $33 in Germany).

Is it necessary to increase salaries in order to sustain the economy? The debate will remain open for a long time yet, even after the success of the Keynesian measures that restarted the economy through demand in the 1930s. In a globalized economy, the increased purchasing power of households does not necessarily mean they will buy more local products (*see Question 18: Where do our products come from?*). Indeed, such measures may boost companies in "supply" economies such as China rather than sustain the competitiveness of local national companies. When it comes to competitiveness, salaries are always a double-edged sword ...

22

IS THE SOUTH BECOMING MORE COMPETITIVE?

Today, everyone talks about the BRICS (Brazil, Russia, India, China and South Africa). Together, they represent 42% of the world's population and 28% of its GDP (adjusted for purchasing power). But does this block of so-called "emerging" economies really exist? On closer examination, besides their size, these countries' economies, political systems and their populations' expectations are different. Some say, sarcastically, that we have the bricks but not the mortar ... To complicate matters even further, a new group has been created – the MINT (Mexico, Indonesia, Nigeria and Turkey), which is equally heterogeneous ...

Even so, south of an imaginary diagonal line stretching from Mexico to Moscow, there is a new, emerging economic world whose destiny is not inevitably linked to the economies of the North. On paper, this Southern block has many assets. In addition to its population and natural resources, it has a lot of money: more than $6.4 trillion in exchange reserves and $5.5 trillion managed by sovereign wealth funds. The question is, of course: What should be done with this money?

From a domestic point of view, national strategies are profoundly different: Russia invests in raw materials, China in infrastructure and Brazil in the World Cup and the Olympic Games. Nevertheless, all of these countries rely on two strategies that mainly relate to their enterprises.

The first consists of purchasing companies abroad, and not only football clubs. In the beginning, more than 800 Chinese companies bought businesses in Africa: It was relatively easy. Nowadays, Chinese companies have ventured out to participate or buy in Europe and the US: Volvo, Peugeot, Addax Petroleum and Smithfield to name a few. The Indians and Russians are doing the same.

The second and most important revolutionary move consists of funding the globalization of local champions in order to transform them into global companies. The result is an explosion of new brands on a global scale: TCL, Wipro, Tata, Etisalat, Safaricom, Koc, Sadia, Aramex, Xiaomi; and in the banking sector: China Construction Bank, Itau, DBS, State Bank of India, NCB, Al Rajhi Bank.

So many names, unheard of ten years ago, have made an entry onto the international scene. Two years ago, China's Haier became the largest company for household appliances in the world, overtaking America's Whirlpool. Advanced technology is also present with the likes of Suntech of China, one of the world leaders in solar energy.

And all this is happening very quickly. Nearly 55% of China's foreign trade now occurs outside of the US, Europe and Japan. During the last 10 years, 22 Chinese and 8 Russian companies joined the list of the 500 largest companies published by the *Financial Times*. In *Fortune's* 2015 ranking, Chinese companies are now among the largest in the world. Companies from emerging economies represent 26% of this ranking, compared to 5% in 2000.

Today, there are approximately 1,000 companies in emerging economies with revenues in excess of $1 billion that can be considered global. Many are family owned businesses: 85% in Southeast Asia, 65% in the Gulf countries. Do we know these companies? Probably not. But we urgently need to discover them because they will be the drivers of tomorrow's growth.

23

WHAT PRODUCTS DO THE LESS POOR NEED?

Even though extreme poverty has been notably reduced in the world (*see Question 17: Is the world becoming less poor?*), it does not necessarily mean that from one day to the next everyone becomes middle class (defined by the World Bank as having an income of at least $10 per day).

For enterprises, this raises the question of how to adapt their products to this population, which does not have the means to acquire the same goods as Europeans or Americans? Many companies have started to develop specific, lower-priced products for these new consumers.

Thus, Tata in India – working on the assumption that 1.2 billion people in the world did not have access to drinking water and that 80% of illnesses were caused by water quality – developed the Swachh water purifier. It functions without a battery for six months, at a cost of $16. The same company became famous for creating a car costing $2,500: the Tata Nano. Elsewhere, Idealab (a company located in Pasadena, California) builds houses for $1,500. Huawei has developed a telephone for less than $80, Nokia for $60 and more recently, Mozilla has launched one that costs only $25.

Mobile telephony is, in fact, a major issue in developing countries. In most African countries, less than 50% of the population has bank accounts. Yet, in several African countries, more than 50% of the population has a mobile phone. In Kenya and Tanzania, Safaricom and Vodacom developed M-PESA, one of the first systems for money transfer via mobile phone. In Kenya, mobile phone financial transactions represent the equivalent of 51% of the GDP.

This market will further prompt the inventiveness of new entrepreneurs. Milan Karki is a young Nepalese who, with school friends, looked for a way to produce electricity in his small village near Kathmandu. He had tried hydraulic energy, but it proved to be too expensive and too complicated. One day, he was inspired after reading a book by the English physicist Stephen Hawking who suggested it would be possible to produce static electricity from human hair. He got down to work and produced a solar panel with connections made of human hair.

Milan Karki's hair solar panels are able to light a lamp for a whole evening or recharge a mobile phone. In short, this miracle solar panel costs approximately $60. It is also made from a renewable resource. Moreover, Milan Karki indicates that half a kilo of hair in Nepal can be acquired for approximately 40 cents, three times less than batteries.

For companies, the major challenge arising from these low-priced products is how to avoid the "cannibalization" that arises in industrialized economies by business models directed at emerging economies. It isn't easy because there is always a risk of "grey marketing," whereby products targeted to low-income countries find their way to more expensive markets.

In management, or in life, it is sometimes difficult to do two things at the same time ...

24

IS AFRICA THE NEXT ELDORADO?

The economic development of Asia these past 30 years has been impressive, and it is thanks to the significant number of consumers who achieved relative economic prosperity. However, this success raises an unexpected problem for companies: How will they continue to use strong production capacities that were developed to serve huge markets? In addition, companies in emerging countries are now becoming serious competitors on local and international markets. It is, therefore, essential to discover new opportunities and new markets. Is Africa the solution?

On paper, Africa's potential is enormous. The United Nations reckons that the population of Africa will double by 2050, to more than 2.2 billion inhabitants. By then Nigeria will have surpassed the US to become the third largest country in the world (440 million inhabitants). Nigeria has one of the highest fertility rates in the world, more than 6%, compared to 1.5% in China. The size of the African continent is just as extraordinary. In fact, Africa could contain, in terms of surface area, the United States, China, India and Europe.

Africa possesses what the world is presently looking for: considerable resources in terms of raw materials (mineral and food), vast stretches of land and a population that is gaining access to the market economy. Africans already spend the equivalent of more than $700 billion a year on consumer goods, and there are more than 100 African companies with revenues in excess of $1 billion. This economic development is at a very early stage; absolute poverty in Africa has only dropped from 51% to 48% of the population over 30 years.

The continent is thus becoming very attractive. It is estimated that there are more than 800 Chinese companies operating in Africa, and more than 2 million Chinese live there. Today, in addition to large mining operations, huge agricultural interests have appeared, particularly in Zambia, Ethiopia, Sudan and Mozambique. These are increasingly managed by companies based in Asia and the Gulf countries.

During the last 15 years, 53% of the world's land purchases took place in Africa; China and the Gulf states acquired a lot. The continent has the potential to become a food granary for Africa and the rest of the world.

For companies, the biggest challenge is finding a business model that corresponds to Africa and its mindset. For example, mobile phones have high market penetration in many African countries – over 100% in South Africa. However, the development of the banking sector has been weak with less than 50% of the population having a bank account in most countries. This situation provided the incentive to use telephones for money transfers. As mentioned earlier, a shining example of success in this domain is M-PESA launched by Safaricom in Kenya (*see Question 23: What products do the less poor need?*).

The lack of national and social cohesion presents the greatest challenge to Africa's development. Competitiveness cannot exist without, minimally, a national consensus and common objectives. This is where Africans will have to create their own model, perhaps by surpassing the limitations of the arbitrary borders that were inherited from the colonial era.

Otherwise, this continent of great opportunities will remain, for a long time, a continent of great tragedies.

25

ARE YOU PART OF THE MIDDLE CLASS?

More than 80% of people interviewed in industrialized countries claim to be part of the middle class. Thus, all politicians want to address the middle class. It is true that the vast majority of people feel they belong to this social class, yet its definition remains difficult. Who is part of it? Who is not? Some of the confusion stems from whether "middle class" is considered from either an economic or a psychological viewpoint.

If we look at Switzerland as an example, the median salary – the figure where an equal number of people earn more and less – is $6,500 per month. More than 75% of all incomes are represented in the $3,250 to $8,650 monthly salary range. In theory, this should be the middle class. In reality, at the lower end of this range, the 13% who earn between $3,250 and $4,340 per month probably feel a little less "middle class" than the others do. Moreover, an employee who earns more than $8,650 a month (18% of the population) or even $10,000 still feels middle class.

The World Bank defines the middle class as an income between $10 and $100 per day, depending on the level of development in a country. Today, according to this criterion, approximately 1.8 billion people belong to the middle class worldwide, of whom 60% are living in advanced economies. The major growth of the middle class will happen in emerging economies. Today, 525 million people are already members of the middle class in Asia. This figure will exceed 3 billion in 2030. By then, the European portion of the world's middle class will have dropped to 14%.

This becomes somewhat confusing when examined from a psychological angle: when can we consider that we have reached middle-class status? To answer this question, we need to look at another concept, disposable income. Economists define it as the gross income minus compulsory expenses such as social insurances, taxes or alimony. In short, it is the money that remains at the end of the month for discretionary expenses: dining out, buying clothes, going on vacation, etc.

In Switzerland, the median disposable income is $27,000 a year (a little more than $2,480 a month). Switzerland has the third highest disposable income in Europe, more than twice that of Portugal, 60% more than Italy and 30% more than France and Germany.

Switzerland's level of disposable income is noteworthy because it represents a little more than a third of gross income. This may be the real definition of the middle class, i.e. when a person's disposable income exceeds a third of his overall income.

This level of disposable income could also be a suitable objective for a nation's economic policy: Ensure that the maximum number of people can choose freely how to spend at least a third of their incomes.

At this stage, people experience a real sense of belonging to the middle class. When prosperity increases, people aspire to have more choices. For them, being part of the middle class also means a desire for more economic freedom. It is also a fundamental component of a peaceful civil society.

26

WHERE DOES THE NEW MIDDLE CLASS COME FROM?

New Delhi: Few things have changed in the Indian capital since my first visit. I met Indira Gandhi when she received the Indian people on the lawn of the prime minister's residence ... Today, my impression of the crowds remains colorful, indefinable and poor.

Yet something is different – mopeds – they are everywhere. These scooters symbolize the new Indian middle class. The youngest child sits in front, then the father, the eldest child and lastly the mother in a sari – four people in all. Of course, only the man wears a helmet! By 2030, 580 million Indians will be part of the middle class.

Shanghai, Nanjing Road: The street leading to the Bund has the highest concentration of luxury labels in the world. All of the brands, luxury boutiques and designers are present. Before, one had to be in Paris, London, New York or Tokyo. Today, Shanghai has become the place to be for the new Chinese middle class, who are urban, hard-working and status-conscious. This ultra-dynamic class is 400 million strong; it fuels a large part of the Chinese economy and it buys our exports.

Overall, more than 700 million people have joined the middle class in Asia, Central Europe and Latin America. They spend $4 trillion a year. And while they have bought some shares and speculated a little to be part of the game, the setbacks of the Western financial community only interest them from afar.

Fundamentally, they want to succeed and consume. Their aim is to make up for lost time during decades of state-planned economies. They want to become rich for their children's sake like our parents wanted to do for us. In a word, the new middle class wants to buy happiness!

This middle class will sustain the growth of advanced economies. It is ready to buy the same products as the Western middle class and, to that end, companies can use the same business model as in Europe and in the US.

Already, more than 150 million Chinese tourists travel abroad and clean out the duty-free shops and other luxury boutiques around the world. The emergence of this new middle class is quickly leading to the creation of its own companies and its own labels. Alibaba, Huawei or Xiaomi are a few examples.

The emerging countries' middle classes will be a strong force that will change society on an economic, social and political level. Quite a few governments are already experiencing it. Through Internet and social network censorship, some governments are trying to curtail the aspirations of this new generation whose economic freedom is leading to demands for more civil rights ... it may not work.

Ayn Rand, the American writer and author of *Atlas Shrugged*, had already sensed it, "The upper classes are the past of a nation, its future lies in the middle class!"

27

IS THE SHADOW ECONOMY USEFUL?

The "shadow economy" is a bit of a euphemism: It is also often called the "underground economy" and sometimes the "black market." Whatever it's called, it is a headache for governments. On the one hand, the shadow economy does not contribute to fiscal revenues; on the other hand, it represents a substantial source of economic growth for many countries.

Professor Friedrich Schneider of the University of Linz estimates that on a global level, the shadow economy amounts to somewhat more than a third of the GDP. Of course, not all countries are affected in the same way: In Bolivia and Georgia, the shadow economy may represent more than 70% of their GDP.

In Europe, the shadow economy is estimated to be around 18.5% of GDP. Here, too, there are marked differences between countries: In Switzerland and Austria, the shadow economy is only 7% to 8% of GDP, whereas Bulgaria stands out at 31%. In Germany, it is 13% and in France and Great Britain, 10%. In Italy, unsurprisingly, it is about 21% of GDP. It is difficult to calculate the real size of an economy that is by definition unrecorded.

One means of doing so is by observing the amount of cash in circulation (in principle, an undeclared economic transaction is made in cash). This has led some governments, such as Italy, to rule that no transaction above a certain amount can be paid in cash. Obviously, credit card companies concur.

Why do people use the shadow economy despite all the risks involved? Some say it is because they have a taste for danger; others say they do not trust how governments spend tax revenues. Probably, one of the most convincing theories is that of American economist Arthur Laffer who demonstrated that the higher taxation climbs above a certain point (over 40%), the less taxes governments collect. When this level of taxation is reached, citizens prefer to hide either their revenues or their expenditures (in the shadow economy), work less or, more radically, leave the country.

Fiscal optimization allows large multinational companies, notably American ones, to legally pay a 5% to 8% tax on their international revenues thanks to tax rulings in favorable territories. However, some companies have taken a different approach: They view paying taxes as part of the "rules of the game," and perhaps they are also feeling pressured by public opinion.

Thus, some companies have adopted the principle of paying what is "fair" in a country, which means paying the same tax levels as local companies. Future reforms to international taxation will favor this principle; i.e. paying taxes where profits are generated and not where the company is registered.

Nonetheless, the shadow economy has a few advantages. When taxation disappears, people have a natural tendency to work harder and take risks – good news. It also reminds governments that when taxes become confiscatory, it has a negative impact on fiscal revenues. Citizens become reluctant to work for an expensive state, and start to look for ways to bypass the law.

As President Thomas Jefferson said, "A government big enough to give you everything you want, is a government big enough to take everything that you have."

28

IS TOURISM A FALSE FRIEND?

Every holiday season, it is legitimate to question the real impact of tourism on the prosperity of a country. According to the World Travel & Tourism Council (WTTC), the contribution of the tourism and travel industry to the world GDP is estimated at 2%, or nearly $2 trillion. This is twice the size of the world automobile industry, and one-third more than that of the chemical industry.

If we add the indirect effects on the rest of the global economy, the contribution would amount to 9.1% of world GDP or more than $6.3 trillion. But is this impact always as positive as we think? Isn't tourism in a developing country a double-edged sword?

In 2013, tourism represented 16.5% of the GDP of Croatia. In North Africa, this figure exceeded 10%. In Greece and Portugal, it is 6.5% and 5.4%. Spain welcomes some 52 million tourists whose spending represents 4.3% of its GDP. In absolute terms, it remains the Mediterranean's champion, and it occupies third place in the world after France and the US.

However, for France, tourism represents only 1.9% of its GDP and for the US, only 0.8%. In an advanced economy, tourism is only part of the revenue mix. But in a developing economy, tourism can be invasive and delay the industrial development and diversification of the economy.

Indeed, tourism can lead to a deadly cycle: real estate and financial bubbles, public debt, the destruction of the environment and it can have a negative effect on the local culture. Unfortunately, in many cases, mass tourism has been perceived as a quick way of generating financial revenue. For some nations, tourism is often counted as an export because it brings in currency.

However, while concentrating on the quick financial revenue generated by tourism, some developing countries have neglected their local industries and exports. And the development of home-grown industries in many larger developing countries was delayed when they became major tourist destinations.

Tourism sometimes acts like a hall of mirrors, as it diverts investments away from more lasting and diversified development. It does not increase the skill of the workforce, and it creates the illusion of economic development, often by exploiting existing natural or cultural assets. At the same time, it delays the transition into higher value-added activities.

Some countries, such as the Sultanate of Oman and Botswana, have become aware of this danger and have confined tourism to well-defined zones. The objective is to limit the impact of tourism on the local culture.

In advanced economies, there exists a growing distrust of mass tourism and its consequences. Naturally, one should not swing to the opposite extreme: Tourism is a perfectly legitimate industry on condition that it is part of an overall strategy for diversified economic development. Tourism is only a false friend if it is a dominant part of the economy, or if it is not integrated into a diversified development plan.

29

SHOULD WE FEAR INTERNATIONAL INVESTMENTS?

Exports are one way to achieve prosperity, but they are not the only way. They certainly have many benefits: They generate foreign currency income and maintain jobs in the country of origin. Exports also make it possible to diversify the economy. David Ricardo's theory on comparative advantages, written in 1817, proves that trading allows every nation to develop through specialization in their area of competence. In such a world, there are no losers.

However, exports present a certain number of weaknesses. Although it is easy to export small products, for example, watches (think how many watches can fit on a Boeing 747), the same does not apply for locomotives or turbines. In addition, an export-driven company is often vulnerable to the development of competition in the destination market. Very often, local companies rapidly try to make their own substitute products.

At the beginning of the 1980s, I headed several delegations of company executives to China. Many European and American managers told me they had sold machines to China, but that they never again heard from their counterparts. When they asked to visit the factories to make sure that everything was functioning well, they were told it was impossible! When they asked if after-sales service was required, they were told, "No, no, everything's going well, don't worry about us!" In fact, the managers suspected that their machines had been bought to be dismantled and copied. They were not entirely wrong ...

Sometimes companies do not even have a choice between exports and investment: A mine or a plantation cannot be moved; you have to go to it. More recently, so-called "defensive" investments have also developed. This has been the case notably for consumer electronics. Western enterprises have had to invest in Asia, not because they want to conquer the local market, but in order to protect their domestic market through the low-cost production of televisions and tablets that are then re-exported back home.

So why do international investments have such a bad reputation? Primarily for economic reasons: When a company chooses to invest abroad instead of continuing to export, it often means jobs are transferred elsewhere. Thus, it implies a loss of revenue for the home country and a weakened industrial fabric. Of course, these investments yield dividends and make the company more competitive. However, at a local level, this is a small consolation.

To make matters worse, international investments were not regulated for decades. It was a jungle out there ... The Bretton Woods Agreement of 1944 foresaw the creation of the International Trade Organization, the International Monetary Fund (IMF) and the World Bank. However, it was not ratified by the American Senate; instead, the Havana Charter established the GATT (the General Agreement on Tariffs and Trade) in 1948, with a mandate that excluded international investments. It was not until 1995, with the creation of the World Trade Organization (WTO), that international investments were again regulated by a multilateral institution. Better late than never ...

Today, international investments are subject to better supervision and play a key role, along with trade, in ensuring that world markets open up. In the words of Victor Hugo inscribed on the monument that commemorates the battle of Waterloo, "A day will come when there will be no other battlefields than markets opening to trade, and minds opening to ideas."

30

SHOULD AN ECONOMIC STRATEGY BE AGGRESSIVE OR ATTRACTIVE?

There are two ways to manage the competitiveness of an economy. The first is to be aggressive in international markets, which means either exporting or investing abroad. The second implies being attractive essentially for foreign investments. The obvious question: Which is the better approach?

Historically, national competitiveness has often been assimilated with an aggressive economic strategy. At the beginning of my research in the 1980s, experts told me not to over-complicate the subject because, ultimately, a competitive nation exported. This was relatively true. All the great post-World War II economic successes – Germany, Japan and South Korea – have been based on a capacity to export. Today, these countries remain the world's largest exporters.

The same can be said for smaller countries. Their objective is to have a current-account balance surplus, i.e. a strong contribution of foreign revenues to national wealth. This is also a way to compensate for the limited size of a domestic market. For example, Switzerland, Norway and Singapore often have a current-account balance of more than 12% of their GDP and their prosperity is based on international transactions.

However, since the 1970s, a new approach has emerged – that of attractiveness. An example is Ireland, which built its economic development on its ability to attract large foreign companies such as Intel, Apple and Hewlett-Packard. The policy that was implemented combined both financial and fiscal incentives (a corporate tax rate of 12.5%) with access to a young and skilled workforce. China adopted a similar approach with the creation of "special economic zones" structured to attract foreign investors. One of the most famous examples is the region of Shenzhen near Hong Kong, which has become one of the world's main electronics workshops. Dubai is another more recent example of a country with an attractiveness policy.

The two approaches have different outcomes. Aggressiveness creates surpluses in trade balances; therefore, it positively impacts national revenue and generates foreign currency reserves. On the other hand, attractiveness creates jobs and promotes the transfer of technology and know-how.

Dubai, for example, has established a policy by which a foreign investor will be encouraged to create a technical college or a training institute for its employees and its local suppliers.

Obviously, the best combination is to have both an attractive and an aggressive economy. Some countries have succeeded: the US, Singapore, Great Britain, France and even Switzerland. Even so, most governments show more interest in attractiveness policies because they lead to visible job creation. In contrast, a surplus in the trade balance often remains an obscure concept for the majority of the people who do not understand how it will improve their lives.

This explains why nations will usually engage in a fierce competition to attract a company that wants to invest in another country: Job creation and political ambitions are the reasons ...

31

WHAT IS THE LONGEST WORD?

For economic purposes, the answer must be "extraterritoriality" (in English, it is officially "pneumonoultramicroscopicsilicovolcanoko-niosis" – good luck ...). Of course, such a long word can only be the invention of a lawyer ...

To make it simple, extraterritoriality is when a nation submits, willingly or not, to another nation's jurisdiction. This is the case for embassies or, historically, foreign concessions in Shanghai in the 19th and early 20th centuries. In economics, extraterritoriality is increasingly a concern. Powerful nations such as the United States are regularly tempted to impose their economic legislations on other nations.

The US and Great Britain have laws forbidding trade relationships with certain countries. In addition, they also tend to demand that foreign companies apply these restrictions, or face retaliation. In the US, the "Trading with the Enemy Act" of 1917 was often used to this effect even though, since 2008, it has only affected Cuba and North Korea. It also makes it possible to impose specific embargoes on products (notably arms) or on people (visas, bank transactions, etc.). Until recently, the US had embargo measures in place against Burma, Cuba, Iran, North Korea, Syria, Sudan and Russia.

From a strictly legal point of view, the United States could only impose such measures on US companies. It gets complicated when these companies are international and have subsidiaries abroad. In law, the subsidiary of a US company has the nationality of the host country.

After the Soviet Union invasion of Afghanistan in 1980, the United States decreed embargo measures. I remember the manager of the French subsidiary of a large US supplier of pipeline components who was confronted with an impossible quandary. His US parent company demanded that he respect the embargo. The French government, however, insisted that the subsidiary, legally French, should continue its relationship with Russia. Sometimes, a manager must also be a canny diplomat ...

In order to impose its law, the United States has a convincing argument: access to the US market. Recently a number of French banks were fined in the US for helping Cuba, Iran or Sudan bypass sanctions. The same applies to the banking industry in general with the application of the new FATCA law. Ultimately, if foreign banks don't respect the new rules, they risk a hefty fine or, worse, losing their license in the United States.

Technology adds new levels of complexity to the matter. For instance, many US companies are suppliers to the European aerospace industry. However, the sale of European airplanes to a country under US embargo could be blocked if the American suppliers are not allowed to deliver components. The same goes for so-called "dual-use" technologies, which can be used for civilian and military purposes, such as nuclear energy facilities.

In 1978, Texas Instruments developed Speak and Spell – the first portable electronic device with a screen that allowed children to learn to spell. In fact, the chip inside was so advanced, notably in voice recognition, that the US Army became concerned that this apparently harmless toy could be exported and end up in the wrong hands ... and used for military applications.

The development of international companies has permitted many governments to impose, by "proxy," their power and their jurisdiction on other nations. In spite of all the fine words, the persistent application of the extraterritoriality principle is often a brutal reminder that, in global competitiveness, the self-interest of the strongest often continues to be the rule of the game.

32

WHEN IS A PRODUCT MORE THAN A PRODUCT?

What do you expect from a product? In short, you expect it to do whatever it is supposed to do. You expect a vacuum cleaner to clean floors, a washing machine to wash clothes and a calculator to calculate ... What about a wristwatch? Evidently, you expect it to tell the time. But is that enough? It's easy to get the precise time nowadays on the Internet or from the screen of a smartphone, so why spend thousands of dollars on a product with a function that is available everywhere for free?

One definition of quality is that a product must meet the consumer's expectations, even when they are unexpressed. You do not expect a car you have recently bought to break down, although this is not specified in the purchase agreement you have signed. When you board a plane, you expect to be safe and on time, even if these conditions aren't explicitly expressed on the ticket. So what are the real expectations for someone who buys a motorbike?

Of course, we could say, "two wheels to go places" but there's more to it than that ... In fact, one of Harley Davidson's former presidents defined the deep motivation of their customers as follows, "We offer a 40-year-old accountant the possibility to dress up in black leather, ride downtown and terrify everyone." When you purchase a Harley you do not merely buy a product, you express a lifestyle, a particular definition of freedom and membership in a group of people who share the same values as you do.

The same holds true for a watch, which for a long time was one of the few pieces of jewelry a man was allowed to wear (i.e. until diamond studs in the nose, and elsewhere, became fashionable). A product is functionality (what it does for you) wrapped in service or emotion ... Most marketing campaigns nowadays focus on this latter aspect.

Let us take the example of a cup of coffee. At the production stage, its cost does not exceed a few cents. At your local coffee shop around the corner, which no one has ever heard of, it will cost you, say, $2. At Starbucks, in a more refined atmosphere that includes free Wi-Fi, you will pay around $4. If you decide to drink the same cup of coffee in the middle of the Piazza San Marco in Venice, you should expect to pay around $10. However, you will be in one of the world's most beautiful places, surrounded by tourists and pigeons and it will be sheer bliss. In fact, it is not merely the cup of coffee that you buy, but also the experience.

In a world where products tend to answer the question, "Do I want it?" rather than, "Do I need it?" (*see Question 56: Do you need it or do you want it?*), the image a product reflects on the buyer takes on considerable proportions. For example, one of the essential functions of a smartphone is no longer just to make phone calls; it is also used to take photos (selfies) or post messages and videos. Similarly, a watch expresses a state of mind, an emotion or a desire for prestige.

How do we convey all of this to the potential buyer? In most cases it is difficult, even inadequate, to do so rationally. Therefore, companies rely on celebrities we admire to "incarnate" the product. It's the famous "celebrity endorsement" which today makes for a number of happy – and wealthy – actors or sports personalities, from George Clooney to Roger Federer. There will always be a little bit of James Bond or Marilyn Monroe in all of us ...

33

IS QUALITY EXPENSIVE?

Quality management is probably the greatest revolutionary concept in modern business. Thanks to quality management, your car doesn't break down the day after you buy it, and your TV doesn't explode in your face. William Edwards Deming is considered the father of quality management. Ignored in his home country, the United States, he left for Japan in the 1950s where his ideas contributed to the revival of Japanese industry. His theory: Quality increases productivity by reducing defect rates, repairs and working hours. In the West, quality was associated with higher prices, while in Japan, it was seen as a way to reduce costs.

For Japanese enterprises, the target for the reduction in defect rates was Six Sigma or 3.4 parts per million. Prior to that, the defect rate for some products often exceeded 5% in Western countries (or 50,000 per million). Such a rate could be problematic, but not catastrophic, for a photocopier. For an aircraft or a medical device, however, it could have life-threatening consequences.

Today, quality processes are in operation the world over and quality slogans are posted in all factories. However, can a concept that changed modern economics also apply to everyday life? For example, five principles of quality management are particularly relevant:

The first principle is, "Do it right the first time." The goal is to reduce mistakes, and the number of times errors must be corrected. I explain it to my students this way: Pass your exams the first time (and when you get married ...).

Second, "The client sets the standards for success." Consumers, not companies, define a product's quality. A good ad for a bad product will not change consumer satisfaction. The problem for enterprises is that consumers more readily express dissatisfaction than satisfaction.

Third, "Measure." In order to improve one must be able to quantify what has been achieved. In fact, it is possible to measure more than we think. A good experience in air travel depends on a variety of factors:

punctuality, check-in efficiency, luggage delivery, etc. Another good measurement is simply repeat business, i.e. when a client buys again.

The fourth principle, "Continuously improve." Once a process is measured, progress can be identified. Quality processes are never-ending: Once a cycle ends, the next improvement cycle begins. Continuous improvement highlights that it is different from a program that has a limited timeframe. An automobile maker once posted, "Year X, Year of Quality!" Very well, but what will it do next year?

Lastly, "Involve everybody." In companies, success is never individual; it depends on a leader's capacity to motivate everybody towards a common goal.

The laws of quality can be very relevant to daily life. They mark the end of the prejudice: "If you want quality, you have to pay more." Quality can be everywhere, and it does not have to depend on price. These laws also teach us that doing things right the first time, and making a habit of doing so, may be the best principle for success, at work and at home ... In fact, it is a state of mind.

34

WHAT ARE THINGS WORTH?

"Price is what you pay; value is what you get," according to Warren Buffett. However, in only a few years, the modern economy has been turned upside down. As a result, the "intuitive" relationship that used to exist between the product, its value and its price has been shattered.

For example, an iPad 4, packed with electronics and components made all over the world and assembled in China, has a retail price of less than $500. But you will have to pay more than $600 for VIP tickets for the next big rock concert. Furthermore, a pair Church's Burghley shoes costs $900. A Smart car starts at $15,000 and a Rolex Cosmograph Daytona sells for more than $50,000. On the other hand, a television set can be worth as little as $120 and your favorite newspaper – no matter which one – costs less than a cup of coffee downtown!

There are many good reasons why pricing is sometimes so obscure. Economists suggest that we also pay for the "intangible," the value that we personally project onto a product: prestige, elegance, group membership, etc. Value now depends more on what the product means to the user than on what it can actually do.

A watch not only tells the time; it is also a fashion accessory, an expression of one's feelings. A hybrid car is not simply efficient; it is also a statement that expresses the driver's ideology.

As for Nespresso, it is certainly good coffee, but it is also prestigious to be a member of an exclusive group of consumers. Celebrity endorsement sells, and not just the rational description of the product – thank you, George Clooney!

Things get complicated with the arrival of the "everything-for-free" market. The new generation considers it has a right to obtain everything for free, particularly on the Internet. Companies and governments disagree, of course. The closing down of the site Megaupload was exemplary in this ideological war. Immediately afterwards, the hacktivist group Anonymous attacked the sites of the American

Department of Justice and Universal Music Group to defend access to "free data" and the liberty to copy.

Ironically, what's "free" has acquired recognition ... In Sweden, Isaak Gerson started a new religion, Kopimism, recognized by the government (yes!) and already counting 3,000 members. Their credo – "The act of copying is sacred – therefore we are indeed a religion." QED.

What is the real price of work? Is it the $3 an hour paid to a Chinese worker or the $45 paid to a Norwegian? Our economy has lost its traditional points of reference for the value of things (*see Question 21: Are low wages necessary to be competitive?*). It's because a series of dramatic changes – productivity, globalization and outsourcing – have had a profound effect on our business models.

It's also the consequence of a change in mentality. The consumer tends to decide on the final value of products independent of their tangible components. In addition, it's because I "fancy" a product that it has value (*see Question 56: Do you need it or do you want it?*) Fascinating, but somewhat precarious ...

35

IS THERE A FUTURE FOR SMALL COUNTRIES?

According to United Nations estimates, India, China and Nigeria together will make up half the world's population in 2100! We are not yet there ... But by 2050, of all developed countries, only the United States will remain among the 10 most populated. On the list are, after the US (4th), Indonesia, Pakistan, Brazil, Bangladesh, Ethiopia and the Philippines – exit Russia, Japan, Mexico and, of course, all European countries.

Size has always been a source of political power. France has probably dominated European politics for a long time because, until the 19th century, it was the most populated country. From an economic point of view, a large domestic market is an asset. Foreign companies are willing to accept many otherwise unacceptable compromises with the Chinese authorities because the ultimate prize is access to a very large market. But are small countries worth that much effort?

Oddly, small countries are often the richest and the most competitive. In IMD's annual world competitiveness ranking, there are only three "big countries" among the top 20: the US, Germany and the United Kingdom. The same trend appears for GDP per capita: Only France and Japan join the three large countries above.

Europe is an example of the discrimination experienced by smaller countries on the international scene. It is largely composed of small countries that have much in common. Of the 28 nations that make up the European Union today, only five – Germany, France, the United Kingdom, Italy and Spain – have a certain critical mass, i.e. more than 45 million inhabitants. Then comes Poland (38 million), Romania (21 million) and Holland (17 million). The remaining 20 countries have less than 10 million inhabitants (we could add Switzerland to the list, but it is technically outside of the EU).

Europe is therefore characterized by small nations whose first priority is to ensure an ever-increasing area of freedom for their citizens and the preservation of their identities. But who governs Europe? Large nations (the Franco-German tandem represents 50% of European GDP) that are often nostalgic for their lost global (or colonial) power. For these countries, Europe is a substitute for international political power, but this is not the case for the smaller ones ...

It is surprising that the legislative structure of Europe only has one chamber in the European Parliament, and has no Upper House (i.e. senate, etc.). This gives a disproportionate advantage to the size of a nation. The interest of smaller nations is always best preserved in a system where the weight of the population is balanced by the representation of the member states (as is the case in a federation).

In the Arab world, Asia, Latin America and Africa, smaller countries are at risk of being marginalized. Without their moderating power, the drive for hegemony by large nations increases the risk of international conflicts. The solution could be an association of small countries, such as the EFTA in Europe, which would allow them to speak with a stronger and more unified voice on the international stage to make themselves heard. It is a matter of world stability.

36

WHAT IS THE RECIPE FOR
A COUNTRY'S SUCCESS?

How many times have I been asked this question? Numerous times! Hence, here are the essential factors that contribute to a nation's competitiveness:

The current account balance must be positive. This means that a country should be able to generate revenues from selling goods and services abroad. The United States, Germany and Switzerland do so. As an alternative to this "aggressive" approach, there is also the possibility of encouraging foreign investments by being "attractive." The latter was Ireland's strategy during the heyday of the Celtic Tiger. However, in a period of crisis, these foreign investments may leave the country. It is, therefore, necessary to be "aggressive" and "attractive" simultaneously (*see Question 30: Aggressive or Attractive?*).

The economy must be diversified. Success should not depend on one or two industry sectors, no matter how competitive they are. Successful nations multiply the sources of wealth. Thus in periods of crisis, diversification acts as a buffer to mitigate the impact of sectoral downturns.

Manufacturing is essential. The capacity to manufacture at home and preserve a domestic industry is fundamental to competitiveness. In addition, a country's image abroad is often associated with what it makes.

Small and medium-sized enterprises are vital. This is the famous German "Mittelstand." Along with large companies, there must be a network of middle-sized companies geared toward exporting; often, they are family owned and have developed home-grown technologies.

Fiscal discipline is a top priority. Without it, governments spend too much of their revenues on servicing debt and not enough on productive investments. They are then tempted to increase taxes, which in turn scares enterprises into possibly leaving the country or divesting. As a result, several countries have introduced a debt ceiling in their legislation (such as the US, Germany and Switzerland).

Investment in infrastructure is key. It should focus on both traditional and technological facilities. Such investments should be regularly maintained and upgraded. A national policy of logistics needs to highlight how best to use them. Finally, the interconnectivity of infrastructures – for example, linking shipping, finance, roads, trains and air cargo – has proven to be a key competitive advantage for countries such as Singapore and the Netherlands.

A scientific and entrepreneurial culture. It allows the advancement of a country's economy towards higher value-added activities to increase companies' profits and the population's standard of living.

A solid social consensus. It stresses the objectives of a country's economic policy and the type of prosperity that it aims to realize. It is preferable to implement gradual and widely accepted policies through consultation, rather than impose – top down – great leaps forward that risk being reversed by the next leadership.

A strong value system. The objective is to strengthen the energies of the nation, give it a sense of belonging to a community and offer it a rewarding future.

Finally, the *legislations and rules* that govern a nation should be clear, simple and easily accessible. As President James Madison put it: "It will be of little help to the people if the laws are so voluminous that they cannot be read or so incoherent that they cannot be understood!" Nobody has said it better ...

PART III: LEADERSHIP

Competitiveness is the name of the game in corporate life ...

37

DO BUSINESS LEADERS THINK?

Someone once told me, "Business leaders don't think – they act." Of course, this may be a somewhat extreme opinion. Nonetheless, anyone who has organized a conference knows the terror of asking a business leader to explain his success. At best, he will struggle through the speech written by his communications department; at worst, he will quote a boring annual report word-for-word. The result is more often than not appalling, yet business leaders do think ... but differently.

Leading a company calls for a different way of thinking. Business leaders do not find solutions to problems, they make choices. In any good enterprise, the obvious solutions are identified at a lower level in the hierarchy. Only hard choices with major consequences should reach senior leaders.

For this reason, many business leaders cultivate ambiguity. This is because they have a strong attachment to the culture of change and they want to preserve their options. A business leader does not necessarily know where he is going, but he is going there. To convince others to follow him, it takes flexibility on their part and conviction on his. Another comment by a business leader that made a deep impression on me was, "I'm always right; the only uncertainty is knowing when." Not exactly humble, but what a powerful feeling it must be to believe that one is always right ...

A business leader's thought process is not necessarily Cartesian. I often teach my students that if they have a logical and rational business idea, they should drop it immediately – someone else will have thought of it before them. Nearly all the great innovators, from Richard Branson to Steve Jobs, have built their success on models that appeared utopian. To think of the unthinkable is part of the game. Hence, the Chinese proverb, "He who says it's impossible should not interrupt the one who is doing it."

Business leaders think through analogies. We all do. When you rent a car, you intuitively know where the controls are. If you walk into a hotel for the first time, you can still operate the elevator. Even the greatest scientists, such as Einstein, used analogical thought in their research. If it works for something, it must work for something else. Maybe this explains the true value of management conferences; by sharing their experiences and drawing on similarities, business leaders develop their own thinking.

Finally, business leaders are all followers of Karl Popper's principle of falsification (often, unbeknown to them...) In other words, "Don't ask me to prove that I am right; instead, prove me wrong." By definition, as long as no one has proved me wrong, then I am right ...

Therefore, competitors always try to "falsify" the business model of the market leader. They constantly attack it with new products and ideas. And after repeated attempts, when the market leader finally succumbs, it is replaced by a new market leader and a new business model. Then the same process carries on, but this time the successful predator will become the prey. Later, inevitably, it will suffer the same fate and it will be destroyed by a newcomer.

All of this is not very sophisticated, but it is how business leaders function. And for this, you need not have read Spinoza ...

38

ARE WE ASKING THE WRONG QUESTIONS?

At first sight, Picasso's statements are perhaps as difficult to appreciate as his paintings. They are nonetheless equally brilliant. Here is an example: "Computers are stupid; they only give answers." I have been puzzled by this thought for quite some time: Isn't the goal of most of our activities precisely to find answers to questions? Our entire education system and business lives are based on this premise. Nevertheless, in doing so, we also incur the risk of finding the right answer to ... the wrong question.

This is what Picasso intended to say when he talked about computers: shouldn't the nature of human intelligence be to first ask the right questions, before seeking the answers?

In economics, there are many examples of businesses that failed without necessarily providing the wrong answers to strategic questions. Sony missed the MP3 impact while continuing to make an excellent Walkman. American car manufacturers did not realize the market potential of small, fuel-efficient cars while still making excellent large automobiles. Nokia missed the Smartphone, the tablet and the app revolution while continuing to make excellent phones. Each time the answer was correct, but the question was wrong.

New companies often emerge because they asked the right questions and the answers they came up with met consumers' needs. IKEA revolutionized the furniture market by realizing that traditional companies were overburdened by costly showrooms. Customers wanted to have access to their furniture immediately – not four months later – even if it meant assembling it themselves.

Low-cost airlines, like EasyJet, realized that issuing advance tickets was unnecessary. It was perfectly possible to function without them; all the passengers needed was the right barcode and their passports. With hindsight, it is astonishing that nobody thought of it earlier.

User manuals for consumer electronics are also particularly unsuited to answering our questions. That is why user forums are so successful – they answer our questions. Crowdsourcing illustrates the same phenomenon. It shows the vast amount of answers and expertise available on the Internet.

Companies increasingly consult net surfers to raise manufacturing and design issues or even for financing new projects (crowdfunding). They often find solutions and are ready to pay for the service. Actually, it is possible that there are more answers on the Internet than there are questions ...

The core competence of a leader is to make sure that a country or an enterprise asks itself the right questions. It does not necessarily mean that he has to find all the answers himself, but he does have to make sure that the issues raised are the right ones. Focusing on the right questions is also a means of ensuring an intelligent use of resources, both inside and outside of a company or government. It also helps bypass the infamous "not invented here syndrome."

Peter Drucker echoed the same idea: "There is nothing more useless in life than to do something well that nobody needs." Picasso would have agreed.

39

IS THINKING DANGEROUS?

Not as dangerous as not thinking at all ... However, thinking too much has its own risks. It can prove fatal, particularly when it concerns innovation or decision-making.

In this respect, the story of Ralph Guldahl is telling. Few people remember him now, but before World War II, he was the greatest golfer in the world, the equivalent of today's Tiger Woods or Rory McIlroy. He won almost every competition he entered, notably two US Opens in 1937 and 1938 and one Masters in 1939.

Ralph Guldahl was a perfectly tuned machine. A taciturn Texan of Norwegian origin, he never exhibited emotion. Another great player, Sam Snead, once said this of him, "If Ralph Guldahl gave someone a blood transfusion the patient would freeze to death." Nothing seemed to shake the success of someone considered, in his day, one of the greatest talents golf had ever known – nothing except too much thinking ...

Indeed, Ralph Guldahl decided it was time to understand why he was so good. He analyzed in minute detail his movements and the way he played. After a period of study, he chose to share his discoveries in a book entitled *Groove your Golf*. It became an instant bestseller.

Unfortunately, there was an unexpected consequence for Ralph Guldahl. After its publication, he became unable to win anything, whether it was a major tournament or minor competition. In fact, he became scared of the complexity of what he had done "intuitively" before. Ralph Guldahl, the legendary champion, was done; he had overanalyzed his swing and thought too much.

A great many good ideas are victims of too much analysis. The "pros" and "cons" kill a decision. Swiss philosopher Henry Frédéric Amiel remarked, The man who insists upon seeing with perfect clearness before he decides, never decides."

I had the privilege of meeting Bill Hewlett a few times. He was one of the two co-founders of what became the biggest computer company in the world – Hewlett-Packard. He liked to say, "If you want to be 100% sure, you will be 100% late."

The genius of many entrepreneurs consists of making choices that probably would not have withstood the "scholarly" analysis of a number of experts. An entrepreneur once told me, "The problem with my company is that we analyze a good idea until it becomes a bad one!" With this attitude, many great innovations would never have seen the light of day. Nearly all business successes are, essentially, unlikely bets ...

Thinking too much can be harmful to decision-making. There are times when it is preferable to take the plunge, see what happens and make adjustments later. It is, therefore, advisable to learn how to live with the likelihood of failure.

In Woody Allen's words, "confidence is what you have before you understand the problem."

40

ARE YOU A BORN LEADER?

Peter Drucker and Warren Bennis are certainly two of the greatest scholars in business theory. Peter Drucker is credited with developing the notion of "management," a rational approach to the organization of a company. Warren Bennis focused on the other great dimension of business – leadership. I had the privilege of meeting them both.

Although they were both US citizens, they could not have been more different. Peter Drucker, an immigrant from Eastern Europe, had a lackluster complexion, wore dark, classic suits and mumbled more than he spoke (a bit like Henry Kissinger). Warren Bennis, on the other hand, was always tanned, had white hair and wore light-colored suits (he was more like Giorgio Armani). Both were exceptionally brilliant, and they revolutionized business thinking.

The distinction between a manager and a leader is the most delicate, and the most important in any company. Managers concentrate on doing things well while leaders focus on what must be done. Managers ensure that the execution is perfect and that the operational results are in line with shareholders' expectations. Leaders imagine and antici pate new products, open new markets, find new business models and motivate employees. In short, they thrive on a vision!

Both competencies are necessary and complementary. However, Warren Bennis often emphasized that most companies fail at both because they attach too much importance to management and not enough to leadership. In short, they are "over-managed and under-led."

A critical moment in the life of an executive is his transformation from a manager into a leader. To become the leader of a company, one must be a good manager first. However, once executives reach the top job, their role changes and they have to reinvent themselves. The metamorphosis from caterpillar to butterfly is not a foregone conclusion for everyone. It implies a different approach to one's responsibilities. A good manager does not necessarily have the psychological profile to be a good leader. Hence the question: Can you learn to lead, or are you born a leader?

Many people would answer that a person is born a leader. Warren Bennis thought the opposite. He believed that a successful executive could learn leadership competencies, and become the one who creates enthusiasm and shows where the company is heading – similar to a captain taking the helm of a ship.

One of his most interesting ideas is that leadership is not solely a body of competencies, but also the result of introspection. The potential leader must first develop his own charisma before he can expect to lead others to new horizons. Above all, he must "inhabit" his role of leader, like an actor, he "inhabits" his stage role. This capacity to embody an enterprise, similar to a politician who personifies a nation, is at the heart of the success of every leader.

Of course, leadership evolves with time. Today, no leader can simply give orders and expect everybody to follow him blindly. As society has become more egalitarian and open, new generations expect more transparency from their leaders and a certain sensitivity to their value systems. Unfortunately, this is not always the case. There are still many "19th century" style leaders around who try to impose their views on the 21st century ... and they are surprised that it does not work ...

41

SHOULD POLITICAL LEADERS
BE BETTER EDUCATED?

According to Tony Blair, "The challenge of Western democracies has always been presented as being transparency and responsibility; in fact, it is a challenge of efficiency. Generally speaking, our politicians are not corrupt, but they don't deliver the services that citizens expect. Our system is very costly and does not produce enough!" Today, many governments in advanced economies spend on average more than 45% of their countries' GDP. Of course, the 2008 crisis and plans to revive the economy have not improved the situation. Budget deficits are here to stay.

The French government's expenditures absorbed 34.6% of GDP in 1960; today, it stands at 56%. The last time France presented a balanced budget was in 1974! Austria, Belgium, Italy, Denmark, Finland and Sweden have already joined France above the 50% threshold. Switzerland is more cautious: The weight of government spending has gone from 17.2% to 36.7% in 50 years, and it still has a balanced budget.

Everywhere national debt is exploding. Many countries will soon have debt levels that are greater than 100% of their GDP and more than 200% in Japan. If the cost of the social security system is included, the real debt of industrialized nations is on average three to four times their GDP.

Of course, this cannot go on. Too many countries live beyond their means and finance themselves through the creation of money and debt at the expense of future generations. This calls for drastic reforms. But can administrations enact them? Governments often consist of politicians, who have limited local experience. The job span of politicians is limited to a few years and, owing to the principle of political immunity, they are largely unaccountable for their actions (*see Question 61: Can politicians decide quickly?*).

In politics, those who are competent are not necessarily available and those who are available are not necessarily competent. Is it wise to delegate half a country's GDP solely on the basis that someone looks good on TV? Would you choose your banker that way?

The administration is supposed to counterbalance politicians, but can it do so? Or does it merely manage its own world where half the activities consist of transferring money and redistributing wealth? Are we considered *clients* of the services we pay for? Or are we simply *administered*?

The sad reality is that our governments function less and less well. It is striking that even the state of California, the world's eighth largest economy and home to many business successes such as Apple, Google and eBay has been on the verge of bankruptcy for many years.

What should be done? Delegate and implement better controls for the tasks the state entrusts to the private sector, like they do in Hong Kong? Educate and pay high-ranking civil servants more, as in Singapore, where salaries are on par with private sector managers? Increase the salaries of key civil servants in certain countries as a means of reducing corruption?

Perhaps. Nevertheless, the core issue is that the administration of a nation needs to be professionalized. Therefore, if leaders are to be paid more, they should also be held more accountable for their actions. This also implies that more money should be invested in the education and ongoing training of administrations.

"If you pay peanuts, you will get monkeys ..."

42

WHAT MAKES A BUSINESS LEGITIMATE?

In short, modern management boils down to four principles: efficiency, change, complexity and legitimacy. The management of efficiency has made considerable progress; productivity has increased and has reduced the price of many products. Change management is often a slogan, but it is unavoidable. As for the management of complexity, the subject is ... complex. Complexity is, in fact, a phenomenon that impairs public and private organizations. Peter Drucker once said, "Most of what we call management consists of making it difficult for people to work."

The last principle is legitimacy. It will be the key debate in the years ahead. We should not confuse "legality" (to respect the law) with "legitimacy" (to conform to a higher moral imperative). People increasingly question the legitimacy of companies and an "all-for-profit" mentality. Management compensation is always a contentious issue. What is the legitimacy of modern capitalism if it is struggling with an endless economic crisis and cannot generate employment? Simply put, the question for most leaders today is, "How do you justify your existence?"

In politics, the answer is straightforward. Thomas Jefferson stated, "The people's will is the only legitimate foundation of any government." In the army, it's nearly as simple. A general is legitimate in his function because he is, well, a general. That's it.

In companies, it is more complex. A chief executive is not elected; he is appointed by the board of directors, or he is self-appointed if he is an entrepreneur. It is true that the board and, by extension, shareholders have a right to control management, but often from afar. It is also correct that the shareholders' general assembly is the equivalent of "the people's will." Nevertheless, any given shareholder only keeps a share for an average of nine months, even less when it comes to technology companies. Thus, does such a shareholder really have the legitimacy to express a valid opinion and make meaningful decisions for the long-term future of a company?

There is, of course, the legitimacy that depends on performance, as defined by Peter Drucker: "The management is the substitution of authority by rank, by that of performance." Steve Jobs was legitimized in his role because he envisioned the Mac, the iPhone, the iPad, etc., and they generated revenues.

Jack Welch, the former boss of General Electric, boasted a record of nearly 100 consecutive quarters of increasing profitability; nobody questioned his legitimacy. There is also an individual legitimacy, in other words, leadership or charisma. According to La Rochefoucauld's maxim, "It is a value we imperceptibly attribute to ourselves."

However, is this enough? As Henry Ford remarked, "A business that only makes profits, is a poor business." For my students today, a company's legitimacy does not depend on how much money it generates. They want a company that makes a real contribution to society and to the world around them.

Nobody survives by proposing only blood, sweat and tears, not even Winston Churchill. Legitimacy is derived from the capacity to foster hope for a better world, and, even, to make people dream ... On *Fortune's* list, the most admired companies are Apple, Google and Amazon. Of course, their products are exciting but they also have profoundly changed our lives. Improving people's existence is perhaps the greatest legitimacy.

43

SHOULD MANAGERS RECEIVE HONORARY TITLES?

Managers earn more than most of us, enjoy considerable power and live in relative luxury. So what could someone who has everything want? At the top of a business career, the most powerful motivator is public recognition and prestige among peers. So can titles and distinctions encourage managers to be more considerate towards society?

Linus Siming, assistant professor of finance at the Bocconi University in Milan and Konrad Raff of the VU University in Amsterdam, carried out a study, using New Zealand as an example. After abolishing ennoblement in 2000, New Zealand reintroduced it in 2009. During this period, they discovered that in the absence of "distinctions" managers had become "tougher" in running their businesses and less sensitive to public opinion. Apparently, they even increased the profitability of their companies during that decade. After the reintroduction of distinctions and titles in 2009, they again became more sensitive to their social environment ...

Great Britain has known about this phenomenon for a long time. Many illustrious business leaders are willing to make huge efforts, particularly for non-profit organizations, in order to obtain the coveted title of "Sir" and to receive the honor from Her Majesty the Queen. The United Kingdom has taken distinctions to a new level, by ennobling those who contribute to the country's exports. Consequently, the Beatles and a number of other pop music bands received a knighthood though they did not always correspond to the traditional image associated with nobility.

Even republican France understands the power of titles. From the Legion of Honor to the Order of Merit or the Order of Academic Palms, France has a wide range of distinctions that provide recognition for those who have made significant contributions in business, politics or the arts. Undoubtedly, egalitarian France likes distinctions ...

The United States offer merits such as the Medal of Freedom or the Presidential Citizens Medal. However, only a restricted number of people receive it. Presidents prefer to award the title of "ambassador" to people who have supported them, often financially, in their campaign for the Oval Office. Therefore, in many countries, especially smaller ones, the American ambassador is often a close friend of the president, and he has contributed to the president's election.

As for the former President of North Korea, Kim Jong II, he broke all the records. He alone benefitted from around 1,200 official titles. Among these were Polar Star of the 21st Century, Protecting God of the Planet, Supreme Commander of the Anti-imperialist Struggle, Eternal Source of Love and Greatest Man Who Ever Lived. Naturally, this impresses the average person ...

Without going that far, titles and distinctions can be a useful and inexpensive way to remind business leaders of their responsibility towards society. There are also countries, such as Switzerland, where it is considered inappropriate to awards titles ... So instead, the authorities invite successful people for a luncheon, which is nice, but a little less glamourous ...

44

DOES THE LEARNING ORGANIZATION EXIST?

The Holy Grail of modern management is to discover the recipe for what Americans call the "learning organization" – an enterprise that learns from its failures and successes. Nevertheless, this quest, which is as mythical as the first one, has not provided any genuine results so far. Enterprises, unlike people, seldom learn from experience. This also explains why their life expectancy rarely exceeds the famous 40-year threshold (with a few exceptions).

While companies have trouble learning, they do show an extraordinary aptitude for "reinventing the wheel." The leader of a large American company once entrusted me with a wonderful legacy – the company's reorganization memoranda over the past 30 years. It was an exceptional document; it indicated that every time a new CEO arrived, he wanted to mark his arrival with the reorganization of the company. More remarkable, the terminology and the objectives were almost identical to those of each predecessor. In fact, to save time, they could have taken the original memo and merely changed the date …

If, as some suggest, enterprises are ecosystems, they are more likely to suffer from entropy (*see Question 49: Why do large companies disappear?*) than to be learning organizations. With time, they develop a tendency towards "de-organization" rather than towards learning and improvement. Business leaders regularly attempt to inject high levels of energy into organizations, in order to resist this "programmed degeneration." Carly Fiorina, the former CEO of Hewlett-Packard, used to summarize the challenge as follows: "Keep the best, reinvent the rest." But what is the best, and what is the rest?

If companies have difficulty learning, it is possibly because they are more dependent on people than they think. A business leader has a relatively short career expectancy – generally, between 5 and 10 years. In a race against the clock, he wants to mark his arrival through rapid changes, disrupting how things were done before. On his departure, his successor will do the same. Eventually, the company will not have learned anything. It will only have changed again and again. How can we fight this "corporate ping pong?"

At General Electric, it is a tradition for CEOs to "coach" the next generation of leaders at the corporate university in Crotonville. By doing so, General Electric has perhaps trained more business leaders than most prestigious business schools. In the same vein, I have always thought that companies needed a "historian" – someone who is able to pass on the history and the culture of the company and its origins to new generations of employees. Indeed, the strength of family companies is often this strong sense of history and continuity.

Thus, it is the role of corporate culture to ensure the permanence of values and attitudes. If this is correct in theory, the reality is that corporate culture is deeply dependent on the leader who embodies it. When the leader departs, the company loses a part of its memory, and the next leader gets busy reinventing everything, all over again ... and the company never learns anything new.

45

HOW TO AVOID JUST DOING MORE OF THE SAME?

Nobody can avoid problems and companies are no exception. One of the oldest banalities in management states that there are no problems, only opportunities. Easier said than done ... Even if problems are unavoidable, the ability to address them becomes an essential element of success in the long run. The errors made by businesses provide plenty of insight. Most people's natural response to a problem is to do more of the same.

Isambard Kingdom Brunel (1806–1859) is possibly the greatest engineer who ever lived in Great Britain. He is considered an icon of the industrial revolution, building bridges, railroads, tunnels and above all, three ships. These ships, the Great Western, the Great Britain and the Great Eastern, revolutionized the technology of shipbuilding. For the first time, ships were assembled with a steel hull, were powered by steam and were equipped with a propeller. For example, the Great Eastern was supposed to travel to Australia with more than 4,000 passengers on board!

Of course, it set a formidable challenge for other shipyards. How did they react? In 1902, the shipyards of Baltimore, in the United States, launched the Thomas Lawson, an unlikely sailing ship with 7 masts and 25 sails! Faced with the paradigm shift put forward by Brunel and his successors, the shipyard did not find anything better to do than "more of the same." The Thomas Lawson only sailed for 5 years and sank in a storm off the Isles of Scilly.

It is still happening today. When an advertising campaign fails, many businesses continue to throw money at the problem to prove they are still right. In other cases, companies are simply over-cautious.

The famous Heinz ketchup bottle has become an icon of popular culture. It was launched in 1872. Everyone remembers storing the bottle upside-down in the fridge to get the last drops of ketchup out. But it took a long time for management to decide to actually turn the bottle upside down and invert the label. Nowadays the Heinz ketchup bottle stands on the stopper. How long did this "revolution" take? 130 years – the new bottle was launched in 2002!

Another startling example is Coca-Cola. Production of its original product started in 1886. On April 23, 1985, the company decided to launch "New Coke." It proved to be a memorable flop. Consumers liked "their" Coca-Cola and they did not want this kind of innovation. Roberto Goizueta, President of Coca-Cola, admitted later that it was "the greatest marketing blunder of the century."

Coca-Cola realized its error and reacted swiftly and well. On July 11, 1985, "Classic Coke" was launched. It only took 79 days to transform a "problem" into an "opportunity."

When companies or people, refuse to confront reality or see that the world around them is changing, they usually get things wrong. Instead of doing "more" of the same, there comes a time when it is probably better to do more, but "differently."

A Chinese proverb summarizes this perfectly, "Madness consists in doing the same thing over and over again and expecting to see a different result."

46

ARE SPECIALISTS DANGEROUS?

It is important to master every aspect of one's profession. But "knowing how to do" something does not necessarily imply discerning why it "must be done." For example, an American professor was a consultant for a large US hotel group. He pointed out to the president of the company that in all the rooms, from the smallest room to the largest suite, closets featured clothes hangers with a nail instead of a hook (so they that would not be stolen ...).

This was sending a terrible message to the customer: "You pay a lot for this room, but we believe you are a potential thief, particularly of hangers worth just a few cents." The president answered, "You cannot possibly understand since you are not a specialist of the hotel industry." To which the professor replied, "Precisely, this is my added value; I react just like a client!"

Obviously, this tale did not end well because the president in the hotel business did not like being wrong. This anecdote is nonetheless a typical occurrence in many businesses. Those who have know-how or master a technology tend to believe they are de facto better qualified to judge what is best for the company and its future. The problem is that focusing on a set skill often causes experts to underestimate change. It is precisely because Sony mastered the development of the Walkman that the company did not anticipate the MP3 and iPod.

When he launched the first Mac, Steve Jobs was not a foremost expert in computers (that was more Steve Wozniak's specialty and Steve Jobs was proud to have taken classes in calligraphy). Although he may not have mastered the technology as well as others, he had a better appreciation of consumers' expectations. The launch of the iPod, iPhone and iPad offered the market what it wanted – design coupled with technology.

Similarly, Lou Gerstner, who was credited with putting IBM back on the path to success, had previously worked in the financial industry (American Express) and in food and tobacco (RJR Nabisco). Nicolas

Hayek, who saved the Swiss watch industry when it was under pressure by the quartz watch made in Japan and Asia, did not have expertise in watchmaking. The Swatch was in fact developed by two engineers, Elmar Mock and Jacques Müller. However, Gerstner and Hayek knew better than anyone else what consumers wanted, and what shareholders expected ...

Know-how remains the cornerstone of success, but it is not enough. Someone can be a good driver without knowing where he is going. In order to succeed, a good specialist must also become a good "generalist." He must be able to understand his environment, and integrate different domains of knowledge, what some scholars call "lateral thinking."

Above all, a specialist must be able to enter other people's worlds, and imagine what they want. In other words, a good specialist must not only know how to do "things right," but also be able to identify the "right things" to do. Unfortunately, this talent is often an exception ...

47

SHOULD COMPANIES BE IN THE COUNTRYSIDE?

I live in Rolle, a small town on the shore of Lake Geneva. Like many Savoyard towns, it features a narrow central road that is called, of course, the Main Street. Life around this central artery used to pass by peacefully between the grape harvest in autumn and the summer regattas. It was so quiet that one inhabitant, a famous film director, used to say that Rolle was "in the middle of nowhere." Consequently, the Swiss Federal Railroads closed the ticket office at the train station and installed an automatic ticket vending machine. After that, the trains passed through but seldom stopped. Then, one day, it changed ...

North of the town, wedged between the motorway and the vineyards, under the power lines, was a strip of land that nobody wanted. Except that this piece of land, 25 minutes away from Geneva International Airport without any traffic lights, was exactly what foreign companies were looking for. A little economic promotion here, a few tax advantages there and in flooded the big names: Cisco, Yahoo, Nissan, Chiquita, Ineos, ADM, PPG, Honeywell and many others. Since then, the bakeries in Rolle speak English to sell cakes and bread rolls to Japanese and American customers.

Are small towns in the countryside more attractive as a new model of economic development? Switzerland, Germany, Holland and the Scandinavian region are also renowned for their competitive small and medium-sized businesses, in addition to larger companies. As mentioned earlier, this is the famous German "Mittelstand." These small companies have developed homegrown technology and they are export driven. In addition, they are not dependent on large, domestic companies, contrary to the Japanese model where small companies are essentially suppliers to national conglomerates. They are often geared towards business-to-business (B2B), are still family-owned and are not quoted on the stock exchange; consequently, they are largely unknown to the public.

What is, even more intriguing is that the vast majority of them are based in the countryside. In the beautiful Vosges valleys of France, there are superb forests and rivers but not a soul to be seen. On the other side of the border, in the equally scenic Baden-Württemberg valleys, where the same forests lie and the same magnificent rivers flow, there are also many small enterprises and jobs. Small enterprises in the countryside increase the density of economic activity and diversify the economy.

Large companies are also migrating to the countryside, but mainly for their headquarters or service centers. Today, many multinationals transfer their headquarters to small towns near airports. The land is cheaper and proximity to the airport makes traveling easier. For example, small villages around London's Heathrow, with their traditional English pubs, have become business hubs for large multinationals such as General Electric, HP, etc.

A new economic model is developing in the countryside where, on the outskirts of large cities, 21st-century enterprises – large and small – are located next to traditional farming exploitations. It creates an unequaled quality of life that attracts the best talent, especially when it comes to the younger generation of executives. Putting cities in the countryside used to be a joke – maybe not anymore ...

48

DO TRADITIONAL
SECTORS INNOVATE?

New technologies such as data processing, telecommunications or biology will radically change the economy in the future. However, we may have a tendency to believe that these revolutions will only affect advanced scientific or technological industries. Actually, the greatest development potential might happen in applying these technologies to more traditional sectors such as agriculture, energy, health or education.

In agriculture, farms have become increasingly high-tech. GPS devices, drones, computing and the ability to manage big data already permit a better understanding of the yields of various tracts of land. It allows better management of fertilizers, seed selection and efficient pesticide use.

This is "precision agriculture," a term derived from precision mechanics. These technologies are critical for responding to the increased demand for food while the availability of land worldwide is limited. The United Nations' Food and Agricultural Organization thus estimates that the increase in productivity for wheat and rice will be between 10% and 12% over the next 10 years. It might not be enough ...

"Smart" homes will also provide a very special meeting point between new and old technologies. Computers and telecommunications will allow better use of energy and improved food consumption, for example by monitoring what is in the fridge. Technology will also keep an eye on your health. Houses will increasingly become places of well-being, interacting with the outside world. Some activities, like shopping or undergoing a health checkup, will partially be performed from home. The gain in productivity and quality of life will be considerable, especially in countries where an aging population becomes less mobile.

Such technologies will also address the basic needs of the poorest countries, and improve their quality of life. It is already the case for water purifiers because poor water quality is responsible for 80% of diseases in developing countries.

This revolution will also affect energy producing devices, such as solar panels and wind turbines, communications appliances, such as $50 telephones, crank-powered microcomputers, low-priced vehicles such as mopeds, cheap cars and, finally, anything that concerns home construction and maintenance.

Media and education activities are also concerned. The advent of online information and Internet-based courses, such as MOOCs (massive open online courses), has forced journalists and teachers alike to reinvent themselves.

No activity, no matter how ancient, is sheltered from such technological pervasiveness. There is a strong development potential for applying modern technologies to sectors where productivity has remained disappointing during a long period. It will happen both in emerging economies and advanced ones. The good news is that "old fashioned" professions will no longer exist.

49

WHY DO LARGE COMPANIES DISAPPEAR?

During the past 40 years, 70% of the world's largest companies have disappeared due to bankruptcy, buyout or decline. Why did so many great names of the 1970s disappear into oblivion? Is there a "curse" on large companies?

The English economist E. F. Schumacher asked this question in 1973 when he published his influential book *Small is Beautiful*. He exposed the inefficiency of large enterprises and anticipated the current trend towards sustainable development. He maintained, "What characterizes modern industry is its enormous consumption to produce so little ... It is inefficient to a degree that goes beyond imagination!" Then he advocated for a world constituted of smaller enterprises, of manageable size. Today, it seems he was right: Smaller companies last longer than large ones. Why?

The industrial revolution introduced what economists for a long time considered an inescapable economic principle: economies of scale. It implied that the larger the production, the lower the marginal cost. As a result, in the 19th century, people deserted the countryside and moved to cities where jobs were concentrated in huge factories. Urbanization became the child of industrialization. The concentration of activities and workforce encouraged interaction between enterprises and led to specialization. In turn, productivity increased and with it came economies of scale. In short, all was well in the best of worlds.

Two hundred years later, another law came into effect – the second law of thermo-dynamics. Defined, among others, by Sadi Carnot and Rudolf Clausius, it specifies that all closed systems lose energy and thus require a continuous energy intake to subsist. This decay in energy is called entropy. By analogy, that is what kills large companies. Large companies need a continuous input of more and more management energy simply to stay in existence. The larger the company, the more energy it needs ... to survive. In short, large companies spend more time managing themselves than they do managing their clients.

The *Financial Times* columnist, Martin Wolf, recently ended one of his articles by writing, "We are learning painfully that some large banks are in fact too complex to manage, too big to fail and too difficult to restructure." Such a statement does not apply solely to the financial industry. It is relevant to all kinds of large companies. In short, are they manageable beyond a certain size? Do they consume more resources than they produce?

Of course, large companies will not disappear altogether. Some are former small companies that have grown, such as Google and Amazon. Others will survive by buying products invented by others and producing and distributing them on a global scale. Small companies have indeed developed most of the great innovations that have changed our modern world: search engines, social networks, video conferencing, online shopping, auctioning and streaming.

The sad story is that many such small entrepreneurial companies fall prey to the big ones. Then, once absorbed, the entropy principle starts to affect them too ...

50

WHO ARE YOUR FRIENDS AND WHO ARE YOUR ENEMIES?

This is a tricky question in private life, and naturally, it is even worse in the world of business. One reason is that corporate structure has changed radically in the past decades, mainly due to globalization. Today most large companies are managed according to the principle of the "extended enterprise" that operates as follows ...

At the center is the "core company" which includes the management, full-time employees, proprietary technologies and brands. A wider circle, around it, constitutes a "first periphery," which is composed of large clients, key suppliers, major distributors and business partners who work closely with the company. Then there is an even larger circle, the "second periphery," which encompasses potential clients, various stakeholders and the public at large.

The further we move away from the center, less information is shared by the company, but it is shared more freely. The goal of the extended company is to outsource non-essential resources, while retaining core knowledge and, of course, profits.

Modern technology provides the operating platform for such a structure. At the center, an intranet is available only to the company's close collaborators. In the "first periphery," an extranet offers secured links with key partners and clients. Finally, in the "second periphery," the Internet provides accessibility to all.

This structure makes it possible to reduce costs by outsourcing resources and even labor. In general, for every job at the center, an average of three additional jobs is created in the two peripheries (however, disparities can occur among various sectors).

This structure is very cost-efficient but raises the issue of identifying who are the "friends" and" enemies" of the company in the peripheries. A key supplier or an important distributor in the first periphery naturally wants to have access to all of the information of the core company. This is required in a spirit of transparency and friendly cooperation.

However, once these suppliers or distributors have obtained technology and experience, they can be tempted to leave the periphery and rapidly become competitors. This is the painful experience endured by many American and European telecommunication companies with their suppliers in China; they quickly changed from trusted partners to fierce competitors.

In addition, it is commonplace for large enterprises to establish a series of complex relationships with each other across business divisions. Thus, they can simultaneously become partners, competitors, distributors and suppliers. These "friend–enemy" relationships are often unclear precisely because it is difficult to define who is a friend and who is an enemy. A new English word has even been coined to describe such a situation: "frenemies."

Employees are mobile and it is commonplace to rediscover former colleagues who emerge later as competitors or clients. That is why most companies continue to nurture and monitor their relationships with companies and employees, even when they leave their immediate business environment. One never knows where they will end up.

51

IS AMBITION ACCEPTABLE?

Unbridled ambition does not have a good reputation today, particularly since the financial crisis of 2008, and a few Hollywood movies ... Nonetheless, ambition, in an enterprise or an individual, is a driving force for success. It is those who wish to go beyond recognized boundaries that foster progress.

Of course, we are not talking about ambition for ambition's sake. Salvador Dali liked to say (with some humor), "At the age of 6, I wanted to be a cook, at 7, I wanted to be Napoleon and my ambition has been growing ever since!" Obviously, not everybody can be Salvador Dali ...

The original word for ambition stems from the Latin *ambire*: to go around, which also means, by extension, to canvas voters. This may have given rise to today's dominant – and rather negative – psychological connotation: a strong desire to rise above others, even if it means destroying them. There are, however, two types of ambition: personal ambition and collective ambition.

Personal ambition is the least popular kind because it often turns into vanity. The ambitious often feed on their own ambitions. They are frequently paranoid and convinced of their omnipotence. Many chief executives think that they are always right (*see Question 37: Do business leaders think?*).

Evidently, it is not pleasant to be in contact with such ambition, which has all the features of outrageous arrogance. But one must recognize that it is an extraordinary strength in life to believe one is always right. Those afflicted with it may be "human failures" who turn into "business successes."

The best type of ambition is one that makes it possible to share a project or a dream with a community, either at work or in a country. This "collective" ambition enables a group to progress and surpass itself.

To succeed, the leader must have strong personal ambition but also be able to motivate those around him. Easier said than done! Franklin Delano Roosevelt complained, "It is a terrible thing to look over your shoulder when you are trying to lead and find no one there."

Too many chiefs are in fact lonely leaders, who have lost touch with those around them. It's as if those around them are saying, "Well done. You are a great leader! Good luck, farewell and let us know if it works." Isn't the "raison d'être" of a collective ambition precisely to motivate people to "follow" you?

Collective ambition cannot be built on the denial of the personal ambitions of others. The era of great sacrifice is over. Those who share collective ambition must do it of their own free will. It is the challenge of modern organizations to have an ambition for the group while allowing each individual to thrive.

Pablo Picasso was certainly a match for Salvador Dali on the subject of ambition: "My mother said to me, 'if you are a soldier you will become a general, if you are a monk you will become the Pope.' Instead, I was a painter, and became Picasso."

52

IS RISK NECESSARY?

Our relationship with risk is ambiguous. Our natural instinct is to minimize risk, even though we are conscious that there is no such thing as zero risk. By contrast, in the world of economics, risk is actually sought after because, in theory, profit is essentially the remuneration for taking a risk.

On June 9, 1865, the famous English writer, Charles Dickens, was returning from Paris by train. In Staplehurst, England, the track was under repair for 14 meters. The workers had forgotten to indicate this to the on-coming train.

All the first-class carriages fell into a ravine, except the one carrying Charles Dickens. There were 10 dead and 50 wounded. Charles Dickens spent the day comforting the injured and dying. He became a hero and recounted many times in his writings the horror of train accidents.

Charles Dickens was a celebrity and his drama became that of a nation. Through his literary genius, everyone lived the tragedy of a train accident. Some demanded that trains be outlawed. The government, however, preferred to increase safety measures for railroads and engineers looked for new ways to improve braking efficiency. The world of railways changed.

Today, our society is obsessed with safety and can afford to manage the problem of risk differently: by removing new technologies ... This is the case with nuclear power. Yet our relationship with societal risk remains rather hypocritical. In 2013, 1,049 people died in China in coal-mining accidents. More than 12,000 people die each year in mines around the world. However, nobody calls for mines to be shut down. They are often far away from us and the world of mines is well hidden underground.

In enterprises, on the other hand, risk is regarded in a positive light because it is the price of success. Making profits implies accepting risk and, therefore, the possibility of losses ... From the contradiction between societal risk (which we want to avoid, understandably) and corporate risk (which is necessary and must be managed), stems the dilemma of "acceptable" risk.

After the 2008 financial crisis, authorities wanted to control financial risk at any cost. It resulted in a plethora of rules and regulations to avoid systemic risks, which can destroy an entire economic system (*see Question 14: Is societal capitalism the future?*). In spite of this, no one has any illusions: Financial hazard is here to stay and companies will continue to take risks.

Thomas Fuller, an English writer of the 17th century, underlined this dilemma: "He who wants to avoid risk at all costs is not safe." The enterprise, or the individual, who wants to be "perfectly safe" rapidly reaches perfect immobility and inexorably falls into oblivion.

The challenge of our times is that society is increasingly risk-adverse while business, thriving on new markets and technologies, becomes more adventurous. In society, risk must be minimized; in companies, it must be managed. Combining both is a challenge ...

53

IS FAILURE THE PRICE OF SUCCESS?

Life is never a straight line that leads directly from early life to success, circumventing disappointment and difficulties. Success is about managing failures and transforming them into new opportunities. Easier said than done! We are all distressed by life's numerous disappointments. To overcome our fear of failure, one should realize that failure plays a central role in success.

Those who have succeeded or made their fortune rarely got there on their first attempt. Most great inventors or entrepreneurs have had to overcome a considerable number of failures before finding their true path. Success is often forged through the experience and knowledge failure provides. It may seem paradoxical to state that failure leads to success. But perhaps more can be learned from failure than from success.

In the United States, particularly in California, I have always been amazed at how knowledgeable taxi drivers are about economic and business affairs. That is, until a friend explained that these taxi drivers were often entrepreneurs between two start-ups waiting for their next big success. In a country of pioneers, it is acceptable to try, fail, try again and finally succeed. This approach is also encouraged by bankruptcy legislation that is more flexible than what can be found in other countries.

In contrast, European laws on bankruptcy are generally discriminatory, making it extremely difficult for a bankrupt entrepreneur to start a new company and find financing. In addition, bankruptcy litigation is often a long and complicated process that unnecessarily extends the agony of foreclosure. On the old continent, bankruptcy is stigmatizing on a social and moral level. Bankruptcies are often deemed fraudulent rather than an honest attempt to succeed.

This tradition may have deeper more philosophical or even religious roots. During the Reformation in Europe, success was considered a blessing from God, who showed approval of earthly acts through the rewards of material achievement. In contrast, those who did not succeed were perceived to be excluded from divine protection.

However, some failure is probably unavoidable in both professional and private life. Thus, it may be better to learn how to cope with it and manage it. Those who have never experienced failure are more vulnerable when faced with life's hardships. They do not have the ability to bounce back when confronted with adversity and they lack resilience. Failure destroys them.

More prosaically, and despite all the books that have been written on the subject, those who succeed are simply those who have tried the most, and, therefore, failed the most. Nevertheless, even though they failed, they learned something new, they reacted and, more importantly, they remained positive.

Failure strengthens character. It is often a necessary path that leads to greater success tomorrow. As Paul Valéry said, "A failure is something which has not yet succeeded."

54

WHAT DOES A SALESMAN WHO DOESN'T SELL LOOK LIKE?

The modern salesman is a remarkable species. Much is said of a good salesman, what about the others – those who don't sell ...

1. The inventory salesman

Armed with pencil and paper, he feverishly checks inventory. Behind him, a line of anxious customers waits until he is done. But it is no use waiting. Nothing can distract him from his task. The future of the store depends on it, and, possibly that of civilization! The client is a nuisance who distracts him from his mission. He dreams of a life without customers ...

2. The boastful salesman

As the title suggests, this one talks ... a lot. He tells anyone willing to listen what is happening in the world, what he watched on TV, what he plans for his next holiday, what his neighbors are up to and what the company strategy would be if he were in charge. In fact, the management listens to his advice ... but that is confidential. In short, he talks to everybody about everything except what the customer wants to know, of course.

3. The suspicious salesman

For the suspicious salesman, all customers are potentially dangerous. It is obvious that the customers roaming the aisles, gazing at the shelves, hands in the pockets of their overcoats, are preparing to do something bad. If a client asks a question, it must be to distract his attention. There is no point telling him that only 2% to 3% of customers cheat, he is not convinced. Besides, since the Greek crisis he does not believe in statistics anymore.

4. The hurried salesman

He does not walk, he runs. He bustles about, rushes from one department to another – he's in perpetual motion. He does not have time to do anything because there is so much to do! A client? "Honestly, you don't think I have time to deal with clients, do you?" And he races off ... to the cafeteria.

5. The expert salesman

He knows everything. He is convinced that he is wasting his time in his present job. He should be at CERN selling Higgs bosons to a crowd of bewildered scientists, who are flabbergasted by his knowledge. Instead, he is stuck here trying to explain the advantages of a chainsaw to inept clients who do not know where the plug is ...

6. The cautious salesman

This one exceeds all expectations in terms of marketing (true story):
Good morning, I would like to buy this product on display.
– I am afraid that is not possible, we are out of stock and I won't be receiving anymore.
– That's all right; I'll take the one on display.
– Cannot do, I need it to promote my sales.
– But you don't have any left!
– That is correct sir, but you never know ..."

His pitying and compassionate gaze seems to say, "My poor Sir, you don't understand a thing about economics, do you?" It is true, sometimes I wonder ...

55

SHOULD WE WORRY ABOUT DETAILS?

"The devil is in the details," so says the German proverb. The smallest errors can have enormous consequences. In September 1999, NASA lost Climate Orbiter after it crashed on Mars because the labs had confused meters and inches in their calculations. The cost of the operation: $125 million! However, excessive attention to detail can also increase confusion. The closer we get to the infinitesimally small, the more we discover its complexity and the harder it becomes to make a decision.

For example, in 1974, the mathematician Benoit Mandelbrot created the term "fractal" to designate a series of figures whose irregular structure is linked to the scale from which it is examined. To make it simple, the deeper into detail we go, the more we lose sight of the bigger picture. Clouds, snowflakes, mountains, cauliflower or broccoli present such structures in nature. At first sight, they appear simple, but under closer scrutiny they present unbelievable complexity. Benoit Mandelbrot used another example: measuring the British coastline.

If one takes a 200-km-long ruler and makes rough measurements around the country, the coastline measures 2,400 km. If the ruler is shorter, by say 100 km, it measures 2,800 km. If the ruler is 50 km long, then the British coastline is 3,400 km. If you zoom to the level of a centimeter-long ruler, the distance becomes considerably greater, but it is still the same coastline, including the same irregularities and the same fractures. There comes a point after which it becomes impossible to distinguish the Mexican from the British coastline (unless it's raining, of course ...).

The same goes for an economy. The deeper one explores the situation of a nation or an enterprise, the more one becomes submerged in complexity and contradiction. Of course, a good leader pays attention to detail. But sometimes one of the greatest qualities is to be able to overlook the details and focus on the bigger picture and what is essential.

The great entrepreneurs, those who innovated with products that changed our lives – Thomas Edison, Bill Gates, Steve Jobs, Richard Branson, Larry Page or Mark Zuckerberg – didn't burden themselves with long feasibility studies to determine the pros and cons of their ideas.

The great political leaders, Franklin D. Roosevelt, Ronald Reagan, Winston Churchill and Charles de Gaulle had a "simplified" vision of the world. Eventually, in economics or government affairs, it is necessary to know how to be decisive and to act on relatively simple assumptions that are not necessarily very "intellectual."

Studying things in their most minute aspects also increases the risk of losing oneself in a labyrinth of details. This can lead to fear of action and an aversion to risk-taking. This is the reason why excellent intellectuals often turn into bad practitioners: They think too much ...

In contrast, entrepreneurs who could be called "rough diamonds" succeed brilliantly; they think less and act more. If the devil is indeed in the detail, excessive focus therein obscures judgment. Details in excess can be diabolical in themselves.

56

DO YOU NEED IT OR DO YOU WANT IT?

Household consumption remains central to the economic activity of a nation. In the United States, it represents 70% of GDP, 65% in Great Britain, almost 60% in Switzerland and more than 50% in many industrialized countries. However, in recent years, a profound change of mentality has occurred. The world of consumers is now split into two groups.

Most emerging economies are in a so-called "first buy" economy: my first sofa, my first fridge, my first motorbike ... If consumers receive money, for example, as part of a Keynesian measure to jump-start the economy, they will buy immediately. This is an "I need it" economy.

In contrast, industrialized economies live in a so-called "replacement" economy. A new purchase does not respond to an immediate need but replaces an older product or service. Sometimes it is simply an update, i.e. buying a better TV, upgrading your laptop or changing your car. This is an "I want it" economy. You do not need the next generation of your mobile phone but you may fancy it.

The problem: Give money to consumers in the "I want it" economy during a period of crisis and they will not spend it. They keep it in the bank ... Indeed, they can postpone their non-essential purchases for a long time without experiencing a drop in their standard of living.

This difference in attitude possibly explains the vitality of consumption in emerging economies, sometimes through debt, whereas, the rebound in advanced economies appears elusive. How many products are there in your house? How many more do you need? How many more can you actually fit into your home?

Marketing techniques have integrated this paradigm change. Companies nowadays manage emotions rather than needs. Swatch was a pioneer in this field. It realized that even though people did not need to change their watch several times a day, they might want to do so, depending on their mood.

Moreover, since emotions are difficult to explain, marketing has used celebrity endorsements to convey such emotions: If it is good enough for Roger Federer, it should be good enough for you ... We all become celebrities by proxy ...

In this new "I want it" world, companies must anticipate consumers' desires. For example, smartphones have evolved into a highly sophisticated machine, packed with applications, from personal assistants to online payment systems, and have relegated phone calls to an ancillary function.

Nobody knew they needed an iPad when it was launched. It was a gadget first, and thanks to Steve Jobs' charisma and power of persuasion, consumers became convinced that they wanted one. It was only later that they discovered what they could do with it ...

A new trend appeared, "Since I fancy it, I want it and since I want it, I'll buy it." George Bernard Shaw summarized this unsparing logic as, "Our needs are limited, but our desires are endless."

57

HOW CAN A GOOD IDEA TURN INTO A BAD ONE?

In business, there are many examples of good ideas that were not initially successful at first. The timing was wrong; the market was not ready. Freddie Laker, a British entrepreneur, started the first low-cost airline, Laker Airways, in August 1976. It went bankrupt with a "little help" from British Airways and others ... Apple launched the first electronic personal organizer, in August 1993 under the name Newton. It was a resounding failure and Apple's president at that time, John Sculley, was forced to resign. Nowadays, everybody flies low-cost and has a smartphone to manage their lives.

The first iPod was launched by Audio Highway in 1996; it was called "Listen up." It was also unsuccessful. Back then, it took 2.5 hours to download 20 songs. The first social network website was called Friendster and it was launched in 2002, shortly before Facebook. Today, it has become an online gaming site. The British firm Osborne launched the first laptop in 1981. It was a beautiful machine. Unfortunately, it suffered from one major drawback – it weighed 11 kg!

All of these innovations show that a good idea is not enough to guarantee success. Timing is essential. How is it possible to get the timing right? A rational answer would be to remain in contact with the market and to know what clients want. This is not wrong. Yet in doing so, companies adopt reactive strategies and end up behind innovators. In the words of Henry Ford, "If I had asked people what they wanted, they would have said faster horses." Naturally, this would not have been very useful for developing the automobile industry ...

Timing is part of the sixth sense that characterizes entrepreneurs. It does not end there. All those who have succeeded in business have something else in common: they did not stop trying and were never defeated by failure. This is what underlies Thomas Edison's famous sentence, "I didn't fail; I just found 999 things that didn't work."

Of course, not everybody has this capacity for resilience in the face of failure. And as we have discussed, bankruptcy legislation, particularly in Europe, unfortunately does not favor risk takers and the entrepreneurial spirit.

The difficulty with good ideas is that often the market is not conscious of its needs. This was the strength of Steve Jobs: "Consumers don't know what they want until we have shown them." Success also depends on fostering a shared mindset between the entrepreneur who launches a product and the consumers who buy it. Sometimes, it requires a bit of persuasion and a lot of advertising ...

In business or in everyday life, the margin to maneuver between "too early" and "too late" is always very narrow. Yet, it remains the window of opportunity for success. It also applies to life. Michel de Montaigne summarized it as follows, "It is an error similar to none, to be right before everybody else."

PART IV: SOCIETY

Competitiveness affects every facet of our society ...

58

IS AUSTERITY A VICE OR A VIRTUE?

There are a few "ideological" debates in economics. Austerity happens to be one of them. It not only concerns the relevance of economic policy; it also highlights a conflict in value systems. For German Chancellor Angela Merkel, things are simple: "Not spending more than we earn – it is surprising that something so simple should lead to so much debate." True! Nonetheless, the definition of austerity is deeply rooted in history and even in religion.

During a conference in Florence, Mario Monti, former Prime Minister of Italy, explained the profound German reticence to revive the economy through spending. He underlined that in Germany, economics is perceived as "a branch of moral philosophy, and [economic] growth as a reward for good behavior." It is indeed true that while many world leaders consider spending or saving as mere instruments of economic policy, the Germans add a moral dimension to the issue.

This debate finds its roots in the emergence of Protestantism and especially Calvinism in the 16th century. Max Weber described this difference in attitudes in his seminal book *The Protestant Ethic and the Spirit of Capitalism* published in 1905. He suggested that Protestantism favors a sentiment of vocation and duty in individuals through their professional career – the so-called "Beruf" (which means a vocation and a profession at the same time).

In contrast, Catholicism leads individuals to think that their present occupation is only a stage on the path towards a better life in the hereafter. In Protestantism, education, saving and work are rewarded on Earth. Success is a tangible sign of the privileged relationship between an individual and God. The economic consequence of this asceticism is that it leads to higher levels of saving and productivity. Angela Merkel's father was a Lutheran minister ...

In Asia, the founding principles of Confucianism are not radically different. Besides filial piety, which leads to a strong hierarchy in society (the emperor being at the summit), Confucianism also advocates loyalty, discipline, hard work, education and saving. The industrial revolution in the 18th century in Europe and the economic resurgence in Asia these past few years are indeed based on similar moral principles.

In Southern Europe, things are slightly different. The term austerity comes from the Latin "austerus" meaning harsh and severe. It is itself borrowed from the Greek "austêros" translated as dry or bitter. In addition, "work" comes from the Latin "tripaliare" meaning to torture. It is thus understandable that the messages of "more austerity" or "more work" advocated by certain government leaders to revive the economy haven't aroused enthusiasm among populations in the Southern parts of Europe ...

Too often economists forget the deeper meaning of words and the very different feelings they convey. Economic policies cannot escape the history and culture that has shaped a country and its values for centuries. Some technocrats have forgotten this basic truth, and they have been confronted with strong emotional defiance ... and demonstrations in the streets ...

59

WHAT IS THE LEGACY
OF CORPORATISM?

For advocates of the market economy, corporatism is associated with all kinds of evil: cartels, price setting, bid rigging, attribution of tender contracts, questionable governance practices, etc. Yet corporatism is part of our economic history and its legacy is not all negative.

Corporatism is a system of economic and social organization that structures a society on associations of people or enterprises. The guilds of the Middle Ages were its forerunners. They managed common interests within a trade or business area, established prices and defined membership criteria. The Hanseatic League was perhaps the first multinational of modern times and controlled commerce in the Baltic Sea area as early as the 13th century.

Corporatism later permitted the organization of nascent industrial unions around trades rather than ideology. This division is still markedly present in Europe. For instance, in countries such as Switzerland and Germany, where there is a long history of corporatism, trade unions are frequently organized around sectoral branches. It has permitted the de-dramatization of labor relations and has led to greater social cohesion and long-lasting labor peace. In other nations such as France, Spain and Italy, with a lesser corporatist tradition, Christian, Socialist or Marxist ideologies have deeply influenced trade unions and led to relationships that are more conflictual.

The economic success of Switzerland and Germany thrives on a fundamental principle: enterprises compete with each other but they also have a sense of belonging to an industry sector that defends its specific interests and monitors the behavior of its members.

The danger is cartelization, which leads to price setting and political tampering. The advantage is that it structures social relationships around common interests such as salary guidelines and job creation. Bismarck's laws in Germany, which led to the development of the social state, just like laws recently initiated by Gerhard Schroeder on flexible working hours, could only occur in the context of industrial and social dialogue inherited from corporatism.

Corporatism was such a powerful defining factor of society that even religion felt the need to take a stand. This was the case with the Rerum Novae encyclical of Pope Leo XIII, which in 1891 encouraged the recognition of trade unions.

Corporatism played a key role in establishing the backbone that maintains social dialogue in nations, and allows leaders to manage economic crises in a more flexible manner. Approaching problems from a sectoral point of view often avoids the kind of lengthy ideological debates that can destabilize countries.

Corporatism also favored professional education. In the Middle Ages, a guild would certify master artisans who could then employ young people and train them in their craft. This approach is at the origin of the apprenticeship system, which is central to the competitiveness of many countries today. It encourages employers to share their knowledge, help the next generation to learn a trade and show social responsibility.

Should we go back to corporatism? No, but we must recognize its unique legacy. Corporatism has succeeded in stabilizing labor relations for centuries. Without solid and steady labor relations, an economy cannot remain competitive and prosperous for long.

60

ARE YOU A NEOLIBERAL?

"Professor ... a neoliberal ..." I have never been sure what it means. Economic liberalism, fine, but neoliberal ... In fact, I don't like the word "neo" – it always gives the impression of being behind the times. Nonetheless, neoliberalism does exist. It is not a step back into the liberalism of the 19th century but an adaptation to current circumstances. In short, neoliberalism abandons the laissez-faire and advocates strict rules to regulate the market economy. In France, neoliberalism's theoreticians are Jacques Rueff and the Nobel Prize winner in economics Maurice Allais; the Germans also have a school that bears the name of "ordoliberalism."

"Professor, you, who are in favor of dismantling the state ..." It is amazing what one learns during interviews ... It is a bizarre sensation because it is impossible to be a neoliberal and in favor of the destruction of the state at the same time. However, for some reason, everybody confuses both nowadays. Why is that?

Simply put ... because all sorts of well-meaning people have transformed neoliberalism into "ultra-liberalism." In doing so, they have combined the ideas of controversial personalities such as Milton Friedman, Friedrich Hayek, Margaret Thatcher and Ronald Reagan. And to make matters worse, Keynes defined himself as a "new liberal." But in English, the word bears a more interventionist twist than in other languages.

In all developed economies, we already live in a de facto neoliberal society. We do indeed have a market economy, but the state is strong nearly everywhere. For example, employment in the public sector represents between 30% and 35% in Scandinavian countries, 29% in France and 21% in the United Kingdom (in spite of Margaret Thatcher). Switzerland is at 16%, the same as the United States.

As for public expenditure, it represents 56% of GDP in France, 48% in the United Kingdom, 41% in the US and 33% in Switzerland! What is this nonsense about the dismantling of the state?

Instead, neoliberalism raises the question of the efficiency and cost of the state. For example, Nicolas Baverez, the French economist, a sworn opponent of bureaucracy, remarks that in France the average remuneration of a civil servant is 11% higher than the average salary in the private sector.

But the debate about the size of the state is closely linked to what citizens get in return. In Scandinavian countries, taxation of over 40% of income is readily accepted because the state is efficient and returns the taxes to the citizens in the form of value-added services.

In the end, neoliberalism essentially advocates for a two-facetted society: the recognition that personal and honest success is a driver of progress in society and that there is a duty of solidarity with the destitute and vulnerable. Obviously, one is proportional to the other: the more you succeed, the more you need to give.

The state must, therefore, bring about and promote this type of society. Nevertheless, it is a "humanist" message that is difficult to communicate. In addition, labels will continue to stick, always on the wrong side ...

61

CAN POLITICIANS DECIDE QUICKLY?

It should be possible, but it is not always easy ... Making decisions in politics is different from making decisions in the business world. In politics, it is necessary to convince, negotiate and reach a compromise before reaching a decision. After that, the administration's execution is relatively quick. In business, a manager decides quickly, but he needs a lot of time to convince his organization to implement the decision. Of course, the distinction is not always obvious; there are administrations that drag their feet and companies that implement quickly. There are also examples in politics of impressively rapid decisions.

For instance, on June 20, 1790, the most famous dinner in American history took place. The host was Thomas Jefferson, one of the founding fathers of the United States and future president. Around the table were James Madison, another future president and Alexander Hamilton, first Secretary of the Treasury. The subject of the discussion was the debt level of the Northern states of the new nation. To support Georges Washington's war effort, they had issued loans they could not repay. They were on the verge of bankruptcy. Other states such as Virginia and Georgia had been less profligate, but they remained insensitive to their colleagues' misfortune.

After a few good bottles of wine, which Thomas Jefferson had brought back from his mission in France, they came to a consensus to restore the solvency of the young United States. It involved asking the new Federal State to buy back the debts through the creation of US treasury bonds. In other words, they asserted the principle of federal solidarity to guarantee the individual obligations of each state. One of the aspects of the agreement was also to establish the new capital on the shores of the Potomac River, the future Washington D.C. By 1803, American finances had recovered and the government was able to purchase Louisiana from France, securing a 6% interest loan with

Baring's Bank in London (*see Question 15: What are the roads to prosperity?*). The United States had regained financial credibility.

Two hundred years later, in the aftermath of the 2008 crisis, European leaders have held more than 25 summits and even more dinners without reaching any significant decisions. Why? Perhaps because extraordinary times – the birth of a nation, a war, etc. – tend to produce great leaders. The pressure of events and a lack of real alternatives compel people to decide. They are a product of their era.

In contrast, today's crises often happen unexpectedly when political leaders are "fair-weather" captains. Democracies also produce politicians who have a relatively limited job spans – less than three years on average. Japan has had nine prime ministers since 2000. Belgium holds the world record for a country without a government: 541 days! How can leaders who are on a short-term mandate solve long-term problems?

The multiplication of actors, often with conflicting purposes, slows down decision making in politics. In the case of Europe, how can decisions be made rapidly, when 28 leaders must often come to a unanimous agreement? Who has the ultimate power and the responsibility to decide? Henry Kissinger is said to have summarized the dilemma as follows: "When I want to call Europe, I don't know which number I should dial."

62

WHY SHOULD WE BE PRODUCTIVE?

Suvarnabhumi Airport, Bangkok. When I disembark from the plane, four people are waiting for me. Going through customs, there are eight. When I am seated in the car, there are many more assisting me ... I feel humbled and think to myself, this is service! However, the economist in me ponders – productivity in Thailand may not be that high ...

It is true, productivity in Thailand leaves much to be desired. It is calculated as GDP (adjusted to purchasing power) per person employed per hour. In 2014, it represented $10.7 in Thailand. By international comparison, Portugal is at $38.7, Greece at $44.2, Italy at $47.8 and Spain at $51.5. So there is room for improvement ... but is this a fair assessment?

There is another figure few people are aware of – unemployment in Thailand is among the lowest in the world – 0.8%! In Spain, although productivity is higher, the unemployment rate is 21%. Furthermore, for young people between 16 and 24, it is more than 50%. In Thailand, it is only 2.3%.

Of course, there is an underlying ambiguity; if there is little unemployment in Thailand, perhaps it is because there is a lot of "underemployment." It is still worth asking the question: is it better to have economies that are more and more productive (such as those in Europe mentioned earlier) with staggering unemployment rates, or less productive economies that employ nearly everybody?

The word "productivity" especially makes sense at a company level. At a national level, the question remains open. When we began our research on competitiveness more than 30 years ago, one of the criticisms of the concept came from Paul Krugman, "It's just another name for productivity." Coming from a future Nobel Prize winner in economics, it didn't sound encouraging. Actually, productivity at a national level can be a dangerous word if it is not associated with other objectives such as employment, social cohesion or political stability.

We have all been surprised to see people in Asia whose only job is to open the doors of a shop for you. It could appear degrading. However, that same person in Europe or the US would probably be either unemployed, on welfare or even on the street.

The productivity benefits we gain through efficient companies are often lost through unemployment and, by extension, increased social allowances. With over 50% of their young people unemployed, Spain and Greece must now deal with a higher political risk, which may lead to all kinds of civil unrest.

At least in Asia, the porter has a job, he is well dressed and he stays employed. One day he too will be able to walk into the shop and do another more interesting job. He will not be in the street trying to cause havoc. In many nations, productivity gains and unemployment costs cancel each other out for the most part, at least in so-called advanced economies.

It may be better to be a little less productive and to employ everybody than to be very productive and have many unemployed people. At least, it is worth reflecting on it ...

63

IS INFLATION ADDICTIVE?

In most advanced economies, inflation has been low for decades. Recently, it has even turned into deflation. One of the reasons is globalization. Competition has increased worldwide, pushing prices down, as companies gained access to extremely low production factors. For example, at the beginning of the 1980s, the difference in salaries between China and Europe was about 1 to 30. Consequently, many central banks, such as those in Japan and Europe, set themselves an inflation target of 2% ... an objective quite unheard of in the past.

In emerging economies, it is another story; inflation remains a threat that reappears regularly in Russia, India, Turkey and Brazil (and in many regions of China). Of course, they all want to fight inflation, but they always have a hidden agenda. Inflation is a sweet poison that is attractive to even well-meaning economists. As with many drugs, inflation provides an immediate sensation of well-being.

For example, inflation is good for economic recovery; it urges consumers to buy now for fear that the price will increase later. Inflation is also a very efficient means of reducing the nominal value of debt. It is estimated that, in the past, nearly 50% of the long-term value of debt has been wiped out by inflation.

It is very tempting to engage with inflation, but the long-term risks are considerable. Inflation destroys the value of work (prices generally increase faster than salaries), capital and investments. Today, advanced economies are ignoring this warning because they are more concerned with deflation. Indeed, deflation can delay economic recovery; consumers are tempted to wait until prices come down before buying, or they will negotiate stiff discounts.

Nonetheless, in the long term, the risk of inflation remains. The volume of liquid assets in the world economy has never been so large. The US Federal Reserve printed more than $2.2 trillion to avoid a depression. The G7 central banks' balance sheets have expanded from

$3.4 trillion in 2006 to $10.5 trillion in 2014. The liquid assets posted on the accounts of the largest international companies now exceed $5 trillion.

This excess in monetary supply takes place in conjunction with an explosion of revenues in many emerging economies. In China and India, salaries have increased rapidly over the past two decades, on average between 20% and 25% per year. Until recently, the price of commodities – raw materials and food – was adding to inflation as a new middle class, eager to consume, emerged in many countries. For example, oil, which for a long time fluctuated between $30 and $35 a barrel, peaked at over $100 in 2014. Although it has dropped below $40 in 2015, it is likely to increase again in the future. Commodity prices are always cyclical.

Everybody is playing games; those with inflation happily consent to this mild addiction while those who don't have any would like to have a little. They all have forgotten what Milton Friedman said, "Inflation is a tax without legislation." And sooner or later, it will catch up with the world economy and bite again.

64

CAN CONSUMERS ALSO PRODUCE?

Today, companies are part of our daily environment. They account for the creation of wealth in one structure that includes R&D, production, sales, distribution and so on. But it was not always like this, and it may not be so in the future either.

The company as we know it today is a result of the 18th century industrial revolution. Of course, companies existed before that. The Venetian Arsenal shipyard was founded in 1104 and was the largest company in Europe during the 14th century, employing 3,000 workers. Further North in Lübeck, the Hanseatic League, founded in 1241 was a real international merchants' enterprise including a board of directors, the Hanseatic Diet. Lastly, the oldest European business with a record of all past meetings is Stora (Stora-Enso nowadays) established in 1288 in Sweden.

However, for a long time they were exceptions. Today it is difficult to imagine that there can be an economy without companies. Yet ... economic relationships center on two models: "B to C" (business to consumer) meaning a transaction between a business and a consumer, and "B to B" (business to business) with transactions between two companies. However, a formidable revolution is currently developing: "C to C" – transactions between two consumers (also called peer to peer)!

Each one of us can create and distribute information without working for a newspaper, by writing a blog, for example. It is also possible to publish a book or a music album on the Internet (as well as sell it) without going through a publisher or a record company. We can also produce energy on our balcony or in our garden using solar panels or wind turbines, and sell it to the utility network.

Better still, the appearance of 3D printers will soon make it possible for consumers to produce small simple objects at home, such as shoes, tools, prototypes, etc., and repair them by downloading an application from the Internet.

For the first time in 200 years, companies do not have a monopoly on the means of production. Consumers will soon be able to step straight into technological innovation and the production of goods, services and information.

Today, an inventor can develop a prototype and seek funding through crowdsourcing. He can also improve his invention by seeking help on a social network. He will also be able to do target marketing thanks to a Facebook group.

This "new" economy will be made up of actors "outside" the world of business. Companies will not necessarily be side tracked. They will continue to provide the infrastructure that allows this economy to develop, such as digital networks, telecommunications or secure payment methods. Moreover, they will seek to buy the successful business ideas, or take over the local or international distribution, and develop global sales.

This is good news for employment, which does not necessarily happen exclusively within companies anymore, but also on an individual level in independent and entrepreneurial activities. At least, this is what the new generation is looking for. The economy will become fragmented and its actors will multiply. This may be what a real market economy is all about ...

65

WHAT DO THE JAPANESE THINK ABOUT?

Japan has been fighting economic stagnation for nearly 15 years now. But it wasn't always so. There was a time when Japan was a real driving force in the world economy. The first time I went to Japan, in the early 1970s, the GDP barely exceeded $200 billion. By 1995, it had reached $5.3 trillion, a 26-fold progression. Of course, Japan's economy benefitted from the great dynamism of its companies, an extraordinary ability to export and the birth of a middle class at home and in East Asia. But perhaps even more importantly, it was due to the exceptional motivation of the Japanese people.

I remember visiting Japanese factories where workers ostentatiously wore armbands. "What is that?" I asked, intrigued. I was told calmly, "It means they are on strike." On strike, but still at work! Later, I saw demonstrations by workers who were angry and had taken to the streets. Nothing different from what we are used to seeing elsewhere. The demonstration was orderly and well organized. However, the demonstrators stopped at red lights, politely waiting for them to turn green. Of course, compared to this, the demonstrations that inflamed Europe and the US in the 1960s and 1970s looked like a mess ...

In 1979, the Dentsu Institute for Human Studies did a survey to ascertain which words the Japanese preferred (a good idea for identifying a value system). The answers that came first, "Doryuku, Nintai, Arigato, Seijitsu, and Kanjo." For those who are not experts in the language of the Samurai, they mean, "effort, perseverance, thankfulness, loyalty, tenacity." Thus, the Japanese value system was entirely geared towards effort, work and perseverance. I was also told that when a child cries in Japan, the mother doesn't say, "Be quiet"; instead, she says, "Persevere."

In 1992, the same institute conducted a similar survey to check if the country's fantastic growth had had an impact. The first words mentioned were (I will spare you the original version in Japanese):

effort, sincerity, liberty, peace and love. In a few years the values of the Japanese had shifted from a system based on effort and community to an approach much more oriented on people towards personal and individual happiness (*see Question 68: How do value systems evolve?*).

I can see the same evolution with my Japanese students. There was a time when each of them dreamed of joining a big company, being part of the "career ladder" and, after a long life of hard and loyal service, reaching the summit to enjoy unconditional respect. No need for a fast track, nor to even think for a second about moving to another company. And women could forget about all of the above ...

Today, their values have evolved and my Japanese students are no different from those coming from Europe or the US. They share the same desire to succeed quickly, to change companies when necessary and, of course, to go on vacation. As for the young Japanese women, one only needs to walk in Ginza – Tokyo's "trendy" district – to see from their clothes that something there has also changed radically ...

A long time ago, an American company manager told me, in a rather sarcastic way, "In fact, the only way we can compete with the Japanese it to pollute them with our system of values." Sometimes I wonder if we haven't succeeded beyond our wildest expectations ...

66

WHY IS ENGLISH SO SUCCESSFUL?

Why are so many countries obsessed with the predominance of English in their education systems, the media or on the street? It is a fact that English has become the "lingua franca" of our times, the main vector of communication in a globalized world. More than 1.5 billion people in the world speak English as their first or second language.

Is it because English is easy? Yes and no. It is indeed possible to converse in English with a vocabulary of only 800 to 1,000 words. But English is also the language that contains the most words. The Oxford English Dictionary contains more than 500,000 entries; the French Larousse Dictionary has only 90,000. English is easier at first, and then becomes more difficult ... So why is it considered so convenient?

English is a language of immigration. It was necessary to simplify English grammar in order to make integration possible for immigrants with little education or language skills in the United States, Canada and Australia. In contrast, French is, at first, a more complex and difficult language. It can be compared to a rite-of-passage regulated by the Académie Française leading to the creation of an intellectual elite. At most, 300 million people speak French worldwide.

The supremacy of English is also the result of the influence of two successive global powers: Great Britain and the United States. The former conquered the world thanks to its military power and the industrial revolution, the latter thanks to its economy. Consequently, nearly all large international companies operate in English today. The technological revolution has strengthened this dominance. Computers mainly communicate in English, and so does the Internet and science in general.

In 2011, 212,394 scientific articles were published in the US, to which 46,035 British articles, 29,114 Canadian and 20,603 Australian must be added. That same year, for example, Japan published 47,106 articles, Germany 46,259, France 31,686, Switzerland 9,469 and Belgium 7,484, many of them in English. Thus, even beyond the Anglo-Saxon world, scientists increasingly publish in English.

Television, sitcoms and YouTube also have an impact. In Scandinavian countries, Anglo-Saxon series are not dubbed but subtitled; it would be too expensive to do so for small populations. From a young age, Swedish, Norwegian and Danish children are exposed to English through their favorite television shows. Today, most Scandinavians speak flawless English.

Switzerland has four national languages (German, French, Italian and Romansh), which most Swiss are expected to understand but not really speak. A former member of the government, Jean-Pascal Delamuraz, once said, "The Swiss get along well because they don't understand each other." The system has its limits and when the Swiss really want to communicate – especially in business – they switch to English.

Even now, the English language is evolving rapidly. The majority of people who speak English today are no longer immigrants, but people who use it as a second language. For English to be understandable all over the world, businesspeople and tourists have altered the original language into a simplified, international standard that is comprehensible by all.

As an unexpected consequence, the British and Americans who speak their language perfectly and who have mastered all its complexities run the risk of not being understood by many people around the world. Simplicity is a virtue, even in language.

67

DO YOU BELONG TO
THE THIRD CULTURE?

Howard Perlmutter, a longtime professor at the Wharton Business School in Philadelphia and IMD in Lausanne, is well known in management circles for having identified how value systems influence the selection of executives in international companies. His typology is both simple and relevant today. All companies share three cultural approaches that determine how they appoint their leaders.

The "ethnocentric" approach focuses on people who come from a company's country of origin. Even when the company becomes international, it continues to appoint executives from "home" to the helm of its subsidiaries. Today, this is still the case in many Asian companies, notably Japanese, Korean and Chinese. This approach maintains a coherent company culture and a closely-knit value-system. The drawback is that an employee who is not from the country of origin will find it difficult to get to the top.

The "polycentric" approach consists of appointing managers that come from the country where the subsidiary is located. Thus, a German manager will lead a German subsidiary, a Chinese manager a Chinese subsidiary, and so forth. The reasoning is that a foreign company will foster a stronger sense of identification with its host country. On the other hand, this approach may lead to a fragmented corporate culture.

The last is the "geocentric" approach. It consists of selecting the best candidate for a job independent of his origin. In a global business world, this approach is being used more frequently. It is no longer unusual to see a "foreigner" leading a "national champion" company that used to be exclusively run by local managers. For example, a German, an Austrian and a Belgian have successively run Nestlé, the Swiss multinational company.

This geocentric approach often leads to the emergence of a "third culture." It stems from living across overlapping value-systems. This "third culture" is a kind of hybrid mix that has developed because of the globalization of business and communication.

At the beginning, the third culture was merely a common platform merging diverse corporate cultures. Today, it has developed into a specific lifestyle. It has its own media such as *CNN*, the *Financial Times* or the *Wall Street Journal*. Social media such as Facebook, Skype or Twitter have brought an additional dimension to the way people in the third culture communicate.

The third culture also has its own dress codes, for some the jacket and tie, and for the younger generation the hoodie. It has its favorite brands that can be found in airports around the world ... It even uses a specific language, a kind of simplified "pidgin" English that horrifies right-minded Oxford professors ...

This third culture has indeed enabled the global community to communicate and develop its own identity. However, it has sometimes resulted in a kind of intellectual impoverishment, like many common denominators. Therefore, people living in this third culture should not shy away from maintaining links with their original culture or becoming more receptive to the one where they live.

The same goes for enterprises. They must be able to combine an international culture where everyone finds a place without neglecting a national culture where people find comfort and a sense of belonging. Being global may also mean running the risk of becoming shallow. Large companies, like tall trees, should maintain deep roots.

68

HOW DO VALUE SYSTEMS EVOLVE?

Value systems evolve with time. The question is how do they evolve and at what speed. Four distinct phases highlight how this is happening.

The first phase – "hard work" – is when a population aspires to work hard and puts in long hours. This applies to South Korea. The average number of hours worked exceeded 2,308 in 2013 (in contrast, France only reached 1,600).

The second phase values "wealth." Here, hard work is no longer an end in itself. It becomes a means of attaining another objective – a higher income. In Singapore, for example, people work hard, but they expect to earn more.

Then comes the third phase –"social participation." In this phase, work and revenue are no longer enough. People also want to be consulted on company objectives and the future of their country. In short, they want to be involved and no longer want to simply follow orders. Japan is currently in this phase.

These three phases illustrate a system of collective values where individual success depends upon the success of the community at large. However, a fundamental change occurs next. In the fourth and final phase, a nation's value system moves from collective values to individual ones. Consultation is no longer enough, people want to speak their mind.

This is the phase of "self-achievement" where the individual considers himself more important than the country he lives in, or the company he works for. His private life supersedes all other considerations. Some have qualified this evolution as "meism" – most people in Europe and the US are currently living through this fourth phase.

From a competitiveness point of view, the phases linked to collective values are particularly suited to manufacturing, where people do their job and do not ask too many questions. In contrast, the phase of individual values is better suited to societies that favor innovation and question established thinking.

All countries go through these four phases. Europe was in the hard work phase in the early 1900s. In 1950, after the war, it entered a phase of reconstruction and wealth creation. In 1968, social participation became the priority. Nowadays it is individualism. Japan is going through such a transition from collective to individual values. The same thing will happen in China soon.

Prior to these four phases, it is difficult to identify a single common value system in a country. This could be the case in many African nations.

Nevertheless, what happens after these four phases? Tomorrow's generations will identify with value systems that transcend national borders, such as ecology, sustainable development or governance. They will share their thoughts through groups on social networks. Their sense of belonging will not depend upon a nation. It will stem from value systems they share with other people in a global and borderless world.

The best nations can do is manage the transition correctly and smoothly, and ensure that legislation evolves in line with the changing aspirations of the people. No state can prevent the natural evolution of value systems from collective to individual, and beyond. If they do, they risk social turmoil.

69

ARE OUR CHILDREN INTELLIGENT?

Of course, they are! The problem is figuring out which type of intelligence they have. That is where things get complicated ... At the heart of the original Latin word "intellegere" is the word "ligare," which means "to bind." Intelligence is, therefore, the faculty to establish links between concepts.

Unfortunately, education systems often favor the acquisition of raw data, in other words, cramming. Helping children acquire the capacity to think for themselves is frequently neglected. Something must have gotten lost over time. When I went to school, there was a poster on the wall leading to my classroom with a quote from Plutarch: "The mind of a child is not a recipient to be filled, but a flame to be fanned."

There are many diverse dimensions to a child's intelligence. It can be rational, deductive, conceptual, artistic, intuitive, etc. There is also verbal and written intelligence. The goal of education is to help children find "their" type of intelligence and develop it. Yet modern education mainly focuses on rational intelligence. Why? Because, it is easier to teach and correct: 2+2=4.

I sometimes ask my students, "How would you save Greece from the economic crisis?" There are several possible answers, all potentially correct. The students need to think, link ideas and facts, in order to form an opinion and defend it with examples. In short, they discover the essence of intelligence; they form judgments and evaluate them – they think for themselves. Sometimes I struggle to follow them ...

The omnipotence of exact sciences in high school and at university is worrying. Of course, math, physics or chemistry train the student's mind. However, let us not exaggerate. To consider that someone who cannot solve a quadratic equation is "de facto" incapable of studying economics or psychology is a little far-fetched. It prevents good minds that rely on intuition to express their own intelligence.

Unfortunately, teaching systems are often normative; they impose a certain type of intelligence on others. In my teaching, I am wary of this. Someone who talks well will not necessarily be someone who writes or thinks well. The know-it-all will not necessarily be the best innovator.

How did education come to this? The idea of anchoring knowledge to the methodological foundations of exact sciences is correct. Taking it to the extreme is absurd. Even the great scientific thinkers never wished things to go this far.

In order to think well and invent, it is sometimes necessary to question established principles and think differently. The Asian nations, that are successful in terms of education in exact sciences, such as South Korea and Japan, are rarely the ones that develop fundamental innovations. Good thinking is only allowed to happen in a pre-established frame of reference.

A logical mind will reproduce the past, yet imagination will fashion the future (*see Question 70: Is math dangerous?*). Does education train children to develop the latter type of intelligence? If it does not, it would be a terrible mistake for their future.

70

IS MATH DANGEROUS?

"There are economists who know how to count and those who count." In the mid-20th century, John Maynard Keynes was already wary of economists' aspirations to raise the status of their knowledge to an exact science. He was right to be concerned! In recent years, most Nobel prizes in economics have rewarded elaborate theories that rely on complex mathematical formulae. Nearly all recipients had a scientific background, notably in physics. The result has not been impressive.

In 1997, Myron Scholes and Robert Merton were awarded the Nobel Prize in economics for a new method of calculating the price of derivatives. The Long-Term Capital Management hedge fund appointed them to their board of directors. In 1998, the company lost $4.6 billion and was declared bankrupt two years later. Nowadays, the Nobel committee for economics prefers to reward behavioral specialists ...

Why doesn't the mathematical approach work? It is probably because economics is mainly concerned with choices and not calculations. In order to manage a company, emotional intelligence is as important as rational intelligence. What really matters is negotiating and understanding different cultures, dealing with environmental and ethical issues, handling relations with the media, motivating employees, managing brands and satisfying clients. All these skills are critical for success and rarely taught. Nicolas Hayek did not launch the Swatch with a mathematical formula. Angela Merkel does not run Germany with equations, though she does have a scientific background.

In addition, the obsession with mathematics ruins the academic life of many otherwise intelligent young people.

Why? First, because of the need for selection: when hundreds of young people jostle for access to economic faculties, it becomes necessary to select.

How? With exams where there is only one correct answer to a given question, such as mathematics. It allows assistants to efficiently mass correct hundreds of copies. Questions, which focus on broader economic issues where different answers are conceivable, require a specific assessment for each of them. Such a process quickly becomes too time-consuming.

In choosing math as the sole yardstick, we continue to demotivate and destroy brilliant young people who are not necessarily scientifically minded. We force them to master advanced mathematical or statistical concepts that will not really help them in their future business careers. Even worse, numbers will give them a false sense of security – if I can calculate it, then it must be right.

Reducing economics to mathematical formulae leads to intellectual impoverishment! It also hinders our children's creativity by making them believe that everything can be encapsulated in a mathematical formula. Unfortunately, the world does not work that way. It is not always rational and logical.

Mathematics is a wonderful science, but there may also be a life beyond numbers ...

As Albert Einstein said, "Logic will take you from A to B, but imagination will take you everywhere." With logic, we will always repeat the past; with imagination, we can create the future.

71

DO YOU UNDERSTAND YOUNG PEOPLE?

As Peter Drucker once said, "Today changes in society have more impact on enterprises than changes in management." Many of these changes are made by young people who shape our society more than ever before. They were the first to adopt YouTube and Facebook. Then older generations followed. Yet, what do they really want?

Access to the Internet, online news and social networks flood them with information. It gives them a false impression of their own knowledge. During my courses, they all have a screen in front of them. Everything I say is immediately checked online and their eyes sparkle with pleasure when they find that my numbers are slightly out of date. Yet, when it comes to knowing what this information means, then there is a marked silence. Professors still have some value to add ...

Their attention span is limited. They would need sixty fingers to handle all their keyboards and four eyes to follow all their screens. It is difficult to get their attention, and almost impossible to retain it. They are often brilliant, have intellectual inspiration, but are often lacking a sense of effort.

They are impatient. Their heroes are Steve Jobs, Mark Zuckerberg, Sergei Brin, Larry Page and so forth. Young people who have succeeded early. They often say to me, "If by 25, we are not billionaires, we will be failures." This may be an exaggeration. Yet, their enthusiasm must be preserved. Many of them expect to start working with a six-figure salary, and immediately implement a global strategy. Maybe not ...

They are minimalists and are always looking for shortcuts. There is no use telling them what to do, they will do the opposite. Or rather, they will look for another faster, effortless way to get the same result. Most of the time, this is irritating, but once in a while, they find something interesting. On the other hand, they often spend more time looking for alternatives and justifying themselves, than getting on with the task.

They do not like large companies anymore. Some years ago, my students dreamed of working for major international groups with far-away responsibilities. Today they are wary of corporate life, which they consider too restricting, hierarchical and impersonal. They are simultaneously individualists and idealists. They wish to work for companies that are ethical, caring and responsible. For that reason, they prefer start-ups and small to medium-sized enterprises.

Biologically, a teenager's brain reacts to high rushes of dopamine and oxytocin. It drives them to seek pleasure in spite of risk and to prefer their social circle to their family. This is sometimes a little irritating, but it is the price of growing up.

We have all gone through this period of life. Let us not forget that during their youth, those who lead us today also broke chairs at Rolling Stones concerts or walked in the nude with flowers in their hair.

In fact, this may explain a few things ...

72

IS THE NEW GENERATION THAT BAD?

At the end of the week, my Chinese, Indian and Russian students come to see me and ask, "Please, Sir, what can we read during the weekend so that we shall be more efficient next week?" I am impressed. My Swiss students – equally intelligent – also come to see me, and ask, "Please, Sir, when does this class end so we can leave early to go skiing and avoid getting stuck in the weekend traffic?" I am less impressed.

Every "older" generation thinks that the new one is a calamity, that values are being lost and that it will lead to the collapse of society. Nonetheless, with regard to the present generation, the figures seem to contradict our first impressions and prejudices. In Germany, more than 30% of teenagers say they have never taken alcohol compared to 13% in 2002. In the US, the number of young people who say they get "wasted" (more than five alcoholic shots in a row) has diminished by more than a third in the past decade.

The same goes for violence. Despite TV and video games, young people seem to be less violent in their daily lives. In 2007 in England and Wales, the police caught 110,000 children between 10 and 17 for a first offense. In 2013, this figure fell to 28,000. The era of "carefree sex" which characterized the end of the last century seems to have ended. In the US, the number of pregnant teenagers has dropped by nearly 50% compared with 20 years ago. Of course, the AIDS epidemic may have changed behaviors ...

Certain repressive measures have been effective. In Spain, for example, drinking too much beer downtown incurs a €500 fine. In Germany and several European countries, the police employ teenagers to go and try to buy alcohol from outlets or bars to check whether the law is being properly enforced. Even cigarettes are less attractive to the new generation; even though some prefer to give weed a try instead ...

This new generation may have lost its "innocence" due to the media and the Internet, which warns them of life's dangers. The economic crisis also had an effect.

The generation of "milleuristas" (those who earn €1,000 or less per month) is spreading. These young people have a choice between unemployment, underemployment or underpay. They are disillusioned with a society that has not kept its promises: "We have studied, we have worked hard just like you said and now we don't even have a decent job."

Generations are no better or worse, they are simply different. The new one is more realistic, more disillusioned and more skeptical about the world that awaits them. They also understand that, perhaps for the first time in history, their lives will be more difficult than that of their parent's generation.

To refer back to my students – after a few months, my Swiss students become a bit scared by the competition from their colleagues from emerging economies. They wake up and study just as hard! Good news ...

73

HOW ABOUT PARACHUTING
A LAPTOP?

Not just anywhere of course, but into African villages. It is the unusual experiment that was carried out in 2011 by Nicholas Negroponte of MIT, one of the fathers of the digital age and the founder of "One Laptop per Child." The idea was to parachute computers into remote villages in Sierra Leone, Tanzania and Liberia to see how children between five and eight years old would use them to learn English, or to communicate among themselves. The hypothesis was that they would get them to work without assistance.

Of course, these computers were rudimentary – they were either solar powered or you could wind them up. There was no Internet access and 85% of the bugs could be repaired by the children themselves. They could open the computers and fiddle with them without danger. The programs were basic and designed to awaken the child's interest in language, writing or calculating. There was no outside human intervention. After a few years, education specialists would visit these villages to see how the children had organized themselves around these computers, and what they had learned.

This initiative follows a similar one carried out by Sugata Mitra, a professor at the University of Newcastle. He became famous with his "hole in the wall" experiment. In one of New Delhi's slums, he installed a computer in a recess in the wall to see how children would use it.

This test demonstrated that children without education or outside assistance succeeded in making it work. They naturally organized themselves into work and mutual assistance groups. Sugata Mitra even believes there is no significant difference between a child who learns to use a computer alone and another one who is taught.

All of these experiments demonstrate that modern technologies can be fantastic tools for education. Of course, there will be trial and error, and failures. For example, MOOCs (massive open online courses) enable students to follow a remote computer course. One of the first – on Artificial Intelligence – was offered in 2011 by Stanford University: 160,000 students enrolled. The limitations of such initiatives quickly became obvious. After only a few sessions, 90% of the students quit the program. One wonders how questions and exams are managed?

Nonetheless, remote education does have a future, most notably in countries where students who live in far-off regions, for example in Norway or Iceland, or in regions that are too poor to fight illiteracy. One of the most interesting consequences of the introduction of technology in education is to show how intuitive learning can be.

Give a young person – even in a disadvantaged country – a simple computer, and he will be able to use it, fix it and start to learn with it. He will need neither an instructor nor a detailed programming course. Moreover, with his friends, he will even figure out how to improve it.

When was the last time you saw your child read a user manual? Probably never! The new generation learns how to make things work by intuition, or by trial and error. We are a long way from the educational brainwashing of the past. Have teachers changed their teaching method? Maybe not ...

74

ARE INEQUALITIES DANGEROUS?

1749: Jean-Jacques Rousseau paid a visit to Diderot who was imprisoned in the dungeon of Vincennes. It was unbearably hot. He sat down under an oak tree, and as he read the *Mercure de France* he came across a question posed by the Academy of Dijon: "Has progress in science and arts contributed to the corruption or purification of moral values?" He declared later in his Confessions that suddenly "his mind [was] dazzled by a thousand lights." Man is naturally good and it is through institutions that men become evil ...

In 1753, the same academy did it again and proposed another essay: "A discourse on the origin and basis of inequality among men." What follows has entered universal culture: "It is iron and wheat that civilized man, and lost mankind ... as soon as it was noticed that it was useful for one person to have a supply for two, equality disappeared and work became necessary."

Today, this same academy would reformulate its proposition along these lines: "Is the economy at the origin of inequality among men, and of the corruption of moral values?" Different times different terms. Joseph Stiglitz, Nobel Prize winner in economics, invented the concept of the 1% – the super-rich who supposedly possess the planet's economic resources and 49% of the wealth in the United States. Who are they? To be a member of this elite club in the US, you need a minimum annual income of $350,000, $215,000 in Great Britain and over $270,000 in Switzerland.

What is the social impact of economic inequalities? In Europe, the legacy of communism was to create a greater equality of income in many countries. Even today, the Gini index (after the name of the Italian statistician Corrado Gini), which measures the dispersion of incomes in a given population reflects this legacy. The countries where income distribution is most equal are Denmark, Japan and Sweden but very quickly we find the Czech Republic, Slovakia, Ukraine, Romania, Slovenia and Hungary. Is this a good thing?

Anthropologists agree that primitive societies, such as hunter-gatherers, were rather equal. Everything may have changed with the appearance of agriculture and specialized labor. Could inequality be the price of progress? In a famous speech to the British parliament, Margaret Thatcher acknowledged that these inequalities existed, but she stressed that, as a consequence, everybody's standard of living improved. Everyone suffered from inequality but everyone was becoming richer at the same time ...

In fact, the majority of the population accepts high incomes provided they contribute to general well-being. The iPhone or iPad have changed the lives of millions of people ... So it was no problem if Steve Jobs was getting rich. What people no longer accept is unfounded wealth. When a trader makes millions on one financial transaction, people cannot see how it improves their lives.

The heart of the problem is that those who have succeeded have often forgotten to legitimize their success socially, through innovation or philanthropy. Economic success leads necessarily to inequality, but it is important to foster a "payback" attitude to society.

It is the selfishness and arrogance of a few that has created the hatred of many, not their success ...

75

DO WE WORK TOO MUCH?

Mexico, Thailand and Korea are the countries where people work the most – over 2,300 hours in 2013. In Korea, people say that in some factories, workers sleep at their workplace to avoid losing time commuting in the morning traffic ... I would love to see that with my students! People in the US work more than one may think – 1,949 hours per year. Most European countries from Sweden to Portugal through to Germany, work between 1,800 and 1,700 hours per year. Right at the bottom of the list is France, with 1,600 hours. There is, therefore, a work gap of 700 hours between Korea and France. At the rate of 40 hours a week, this represents 17 weeks or more than four months per year ...

It has not always been this way. Europe and the US were once the "Koreans" of their time. The industrial revolution in the 19th century and the economic boom at the beginning of the 20th century was built on hard work. In the United States, it was not until August 3, 1923, that an agreement in the steel industry limited a working day to 12 hours, 6 days a week! Beforehand, President Harding had to deploy his influence to overcome the reluctance of employers who, already then, feared the collapse of US competitiveness.

Seventeen countries in the world still work more than 2,000 hours per year. At the bottom of the list Portugal, Denmark and France work less than 1,700 hours per year. However, does the number of working hours increase productivity? Not when it comes to innovation. The US works 350 hours less than Korea but, as of 2014, it had won 283 Nobel prizes in physics, chemistry, medicine and economics; Korea has not been awarded one yet.

Nonetheless, below a certain number of working hours, it becomes difficult for a state to fund a decent social security and health system. Tax revenues also depend on the size of the workforce. This is called the rate of employment. In Switzerland, total employment represents more than 58% of the population. In Germany, it is 51%. Unfortunately, in France, it is only 43%.

If a nation has fewer people actively employed, it has little choice but to finance the state's standard of living through heavy taxation of the "happy few" who are employed. Indeed, the great advantage of having a wider population base at work is that a nation can afford to maintain lower tax rates while still collecting sufficient fiscal revenues.

The unexpected consequence, as illustrated by France, is that when the total number of people employed is lower, they are generally more productive. Looking at the GDP per person employed (a simple measure of national productivity), France exceeds $55 per hour, one of the highest levels per capita in the world! Unfortunately, for these very productive, and thus very valuable, French, they pay considerable taxes, so that their government can continue to spend more than 56% of national GDP.

Even if it is advisable to work well rather than to work a lot, a country cannot escape from the necessity of working a minimum number of hours. This is the only way to ensure that a population can afford and benefit from the social structure it wants – health, education and a pension system. The number of working hours and a large employed population is thus critical to maintaining a decent standard of living in a nation. Even if demographics imply an increase in the number of dependent persons, people at work should not become a rarity ...

76

IS WATER TOMORROW'S BLUE GOLD?

Few resources on Earth are as abundant as water; yet none is so unequally distributed, so valuable and yet so undervalued. The greatest economic and ecological debate of the 21st century will probably center on water. The oceans' water (1,351 billion km³) covers the greater part of the planet. Yet it is salty. Most freshwater resources (69%) are locked in glaciers and in the ice caps at the poles. Fresh water available for agriculture and human consumption accounts for only 2.5% of global supply (35 million km³).

Access to fresh water remains a privilege. Ten countries hold 60% of the world's freshwater resources; among them are Brazil, Russia, the United States, China and Canada. Per capita, Switzerland is at the top of the list due to its many lakes and glaciers. For the 13% of the world's population who live below the absolute poverty level, getting drinking water, together with food and heating materials, is the main activity of each day. As mentioned earlier, poor water quality accounts for 90% of the diseases in poor countries.

Yet water consumption is increasing. Globally, it was around 1,000 km³ per year in 1940; nowadays, it exceeds 4,200 km³ and it will reach 5,000 km³ by 2025. Agriculture is responsible for 70% of the world's water consumption, industry for 22% and households for a mere 8%. Revenue disparities have a huge impact; in East Asia, 80% of water consumption is still used for agriculture; in Western Europe, it is only 22%. Moreover, changes in eating habits affect these figures considerably. By 2030, beef consumption will have increased by 85%, according to the World Bank. Yet, total production of a kilo of beef consumes nearly 15,000 liters of water.

Gaining access to good quality water has become a priority. There was an imaginative project to haul an iceberg toward the Gulf countries for the water it would supply when it melted. Desalinization techniques seem a more realistic solution. Today, more than 17,000 factories desalinize approximately 80 million m³ of water per day, 10 times more than in 1980. Companies such as Nestlé, Unilever and Tata in India have embarked on the production of cheap water purifiers for urban households in developing countries.

Aquaculture will also make it possible to satisfy humanity's new protein needs. Currently, 88% of fish stocks in Europe are over-fished. In Nova Scotia, fishermen use four times more fuel per ton of fish than 50 years ago, i.e. 30 liters. Their European colleagues must sail further out and consume 100 liters of fuel per ton.

Therefore, shifting from wild fishing to fish farming is becoming a necessity for humanity. The good news, however, is that since 2013, production of fish from fish farms exceeds catches from the open oceans.

However, it's our behaviors that will have to change the most. We must start viewing water, which is an obvious and available resource for many of us, as rare and precious.

Thus, we will have to change our attitudes. For example, until very recently, there was no charge for water usage in Ireland. As a consequence, the water consumption per person is 386 liters per day, two to three times more than in other European countries. Without adequate revenues to repair delivery pipes, 41% of them are leaking. Water is indeed the blue gold and we should consider it as such. And maybe, one day, we should also stop watering our plants with drinking water ...

77

SHOULD WE EAT OUR DOG?

The title of this chapter is drawn from a book written by Robert and Brenda Vale of Wellington University in New Zealand. Great marketing! Fundamentally, it provides *food* for thought; our four-legged friends have a more important ecological footprint than we think. In short, they are the unexpected polluters of our planet. And their impact is bigger than one would think ...

The figures are overwhelming: a mid-sized dog consumes 164 kg of meat and 95 kg of cereal per year. Since it takes 43.3 m² of land to produce 1 kg of chicken and 13.4 m² of land for 1 kg of cereals, our four-legged friends have an ecological footprint of 0.84 hectares a year. If you own a bigger dog like a German shepherd, this figure rises to 1.1 hectares.

And it gets more interesting. The Vales have compared these results with a 4.6-liter Toyota Land Cruiser driven 10,000 km a year. This car – frowned upon by many environmentalists – consumes 55.1 gigajoules per year of energy, including fuel and its manufacture. In ecological footprint terms, this corresponds to 0.41 hectares, half that of a mid-sized dog and nearly one-third that of a larger dog. Overall, someone who takes the train with his dog pollutes more than somebody who goes to the office in a 4x4. Nobody had ever thought about it (and these figures have been checked by *New Scientist* magazine).

If you are not a "dog" but a "cat" lover, do not get excited too quickly. In Great Britain, 7.7 million cats kill on average 188 million wild animals per year or 25 per cat. In the US, there are 76 million cats; thus, it is easy to imagine the slaughter ... Who would have thought that the furry balls that purr tenderly on your lap, behave like hooligans once outside?

This is a prime example of the law of unintended consequences, which can apply to dogs, cats, the environment and the economy. Nowadays, systems are so interlinked with each other that it is practically impossible to control all the consequences along the chain of events.

The "Body Shop" had built up a justified reputation for guaranteeing that its products respected the environment and did not use animal testing. Unfortunately, they discovered that suppliers, or suppliers of suppliers, did not respect their commitment entirely. It was a blow to the company's image, its employees and, of course, its customers!

The complexity of our economic environment is such that, today, no one can foresee every consequence – expected or not – of our policies in ecology, nutrition, energy or finance.

Uncompromising virtue and infallibility do not exist, except in religion, perhaps … A little humility is a good daily practice.

I will have to stop here; my dog Shamrock is giving me worried looks. No, I will not be eating her this evening …

PART V: YOU

Competitiveness is also a matter of mindset ...

78

HOW MANY FRIENDS DO YOU NEED?

One is enough if it is the right one ... The work of Robin Dunbar, an anthropologist at the University of Oxford and his colleague Russell Hill can shed light on this question. Is the mind programmed to manage only a preset number of contacts? Homo sapiens (us) have the ability to manage relationships in a group through language, work, commerce and exchange of knowledge. In the era of Facebook and Twitter, how big is the modern "tribe" we depend on for success?

At the outset, Dunbar and Hill started with a brilliant and simple idea: how many Christmas cards did a typical British family send 20 years ago? Sending greetings at the end of the year takes time and effort: buying the cards, finding the addresses, etc. It is, therefore, limited to essential contacts: 25% to family, 60% to friends and the rest to colleagues. Surprisingly, the total number was relatively even across Britain: 153.5 cards!

This figure of about 150 seems to be etched into our brains. Anthropologists calculate that the first villages consisted of about 150 people. In most armies, the smallest unit is the "company" which is made up of around 150 men. Enterprises have a natural tendency to split business units when they exceed this number, above which it is difficult to remember everybody's name and face. This "150" is indeed found in many "spontaneous" structures around us. Hence, it became "the Dunbar number."

But what about today with the Internet? The Pew Research Center reckons that 65% of American adults use social networking sites today. A teenager in the United States has an average of 79 regular contacts on Twitter, and 300 friends on Facebook. However, on average, a typical Facebook user has 145 friends – back to the Dunbar number ...

Indeed, it is easier to multiply contacts than to manage them. Political figures or entertainment celebrities have thousands of "friends" on social media. But what are these contacts worth? Isn't the real value of a Christmas card the effort it requires and the implied personal attention? Those who send cards in large numbers or print them by the thousand can save a lot of money. They have no value for the receiver and go directly into the wastebasket.

We certainly need friends and business contacts to develop our private lives and to succeed professionally. Our brain, which is initially programmed to deal with a number of around 150, finds it difficult to cope with more. How many business meetings or dinners with friends can you organize properly in a year and still devote the necessary attention to your guests?

"Properly" is the key word; more does not necessarily mean better. For those who experienced the pre-Facebook era, the concept of limiting contacts and making choices is relatively normal. For the younger generation, it would be more difficult because a large number of contacts have always been a reality.

For many, the number of contacts gathered is a status symbol. I am successful because I have many contacts, even if I do not know who they are. For others, contacts are friends and should be treated as a luxury for which exclusivity and rarity also create special value. Indeed, it is your choice.

79

ARE PEOPLE EASILY DECEIVED?

In his book *The Democracy of the Gullible* Professor Gérald Bronner of the University of Paris Diderot, shows how the Internet reinforces weird ideas. Point in fact – search engines are only following an already well-established pattern. If you believe that the CIA was responsible for the September 11 attacks, you will find many ideas to strengthen your theory in your search engine's first 60 results (the ones that are most read). If you are a believer in the conspiracy theory about the same attacks, you will find more than 100 different arguments – from a seismic fault to extraterrestrials – that will reinforce your conviction.

Not everyone lacks a critical mind. The unexpected consequence of search engines is to provide arguments for the craziest ideas. Fear causes credulity, and credulity feeds on these so-called "facts" on the Internet. Today, anyone can slander companies, governments and individuals by pretending to be wise through knowledge gleaned on the Internet. Whatever you think, you will always find someone on the web to prove you right ... The expert citizen is born! Experts that are easily fooled ...

At the origin of this gullibility is fear – fear of the world around us, the economic crisis and the belief that the government hides everything from us and knows everything about us. Because of these suspicions, there are many who turn to the web in search of answers to their anguish and the comfort of knowing that there are others who share it.

The election of Pope Francis highlights the ambiguity of our times. The Catholic Church is criticized from all sides for its ultra-conservative positions and its denial of many scandals. Yet, when it came to the announcement of a new pope, the population held its breath and media from all over the world took St. Peter's Square by storm. Why?

While awaiting the announcement of the new Pope, I recalled the first speech of John-Paul II on October 22, 1978, which began with these words: "Do not be afraid ...." Thus, as the economy spreads fear of a future that could be worse than the present, religion, and not just the Catholic Church, returns to its original message of hope. The decline of the Catholic Church began the day a message of authority and terror replaced the hope of the early years when being a Christian meant fighting fear together. It ultimately led to the Inquisition.

Does the modern economy follow the same path? Has "Progress, calm and strong, and always innocent ...," as proclaimed by Victor Hugo, been replaced by fear of job losses and the pressures of work? Has confidence in a better future given way to the fear of tomorrow? If it cannot manage hope, today's economy will lose its legitimacy and people will continue to believe in far-fetched theories on the web, in an attempt to find comfort and partners in distress.

When people are afraid they are willing to believe anything and anyone. Online debates on social media often resemble collective psychodramas. Often an endless discussion goes round and round in circles giving the impression of desperation. Leaders – in politics and economics – should help people master their fear of the future and calmly confront the challenges of tomorrow.

As Napoleon once said: "One can only lead people by showing them the way to a better future."

80

FAMOUS OR INFAMOUS ON THE INTERNET?

"It takes so long to create a reputation and so little to lose it." These words come from Thomas Watson Jr., founder of IBM. In fact, nothing is harder than building a positive image for an enterprise, or for oneself. Moreover, it can vanish from one day to the next. In the past, a good reputation was built within a small circle. Newspapers widened that circle, and television has made it possible to promote a national, and in some cases, an international reputation. However, the greatest revolution has come from the Internet and social media. They have enabled the creation of a truly global image. Yet ...

Andy Warhol once said, "In the future, everyone will be world-famous for 15 minutes." This is exactly what is happening today with social networks and YouTube. Everyone aspires to fame for a few minutes and is ready to do almost anything to get it. Their reputations, however, may suffer from long-lasting damage. It is practically impossible to erase one's tracks on the Internet (even though "the right to be forgotten" is a concept that is on the move).

Today, the practice of checking a person's profile on search engines or social media has become a common practice in human resource departments. Sometimes a youthful misstep or being in the wrong place at the wrong time can result in a negative image. Whatever the reason, a negative image may follow you all your life.

The same goes for enterprises. They are finding their reputations increasingly difficult to manage on the Internet. Only recently, a major beer brand sponsored a folk festival in Mongolia. After the festival was over, instead of shipping the advertising posters home, the company managers left them on site. Unfortunately, the following day, a deadly dogfighting competition took place ... Someone took a video with their mobile phone, posted it on the Internet and spread the rumor that the company sponsored gory dogfights. It took the brewer months to restore its reputation.

A good reputation, for a company or an individual, is built every day and unfailingly. As Mark Twain said, "Don't do anything wrong, particularly if someone is watching." Today, with the Internet, everybody is watching. In fact, there are two possibilities: either be totally absent from the Internet and social networks, on the assumption that "a life hidden is a happy life," or be extremely active by taking the initiative and spending a considerable amount of time on it.

In both cases, managing an image becomes a time-consuming activity, both for enterprises and for individuals. However, eventually, it is more or less impossible to avoid becoming a victim of slander.

Therefore, managing one's reputation also means managing one's bad reputation. Politicians have experienced this for a long time. Companies are discovering it. Individuals are a lot less prepared. Offensive remarks are obviously perceived as insulting. This is the price to pay for those who want a brief moment of fame; movie stars know that the cost of visibility is often slander.

Of course, there is always the possibility of ignoring this and becoming a recluse. Following the advice of Mark Twain, happiness may be "a good book and a clear conscience."

81

ARE YOU MOBILE?

In cities, mobility is disappearing. At certain times of the day, Amsterdam, Dubai, Dublin, Geneva, London, New York and Shanghai stop moving. Drivers are stuck in traffic jams, train stations are packed, taxis and buses are taken by storm, air traffic is overloaded, delays pile up and waiting lines get longer. At a time when mobility is a primary virtue in a modern economy, it is ironic that as cities expand, people are less likely to move ...

The trend will continue as cities become increasingly predominant in our environment. In the past 100 years, the urban population has grown from 150 million to 3 billion! Some urban agglomerations are colossal: Tokyo-Yokoyama has 37 million inhabitants; Delhi, Manila and Seoul have 24 million, Beijing, Mexico and New York have 21 million.

The United Nations estimates that, by 2030, nearly 60% of the world's population will live in cities. In smaller countries such as Switzerland, already more than two-thirds of the population is living in urban areas.

A new trend emerges. Agglomerations of urban areas, so-called mega-regions, are developing all over the world. For example, the Pearl River Delta in Southern China already counts 120 million people around Hong Kong, Macao, Shenzhen and Guangzhou. In Japan, 60 million people live in the mega-region of Osaka, Kobe, Nagoya and Kyoto. Two-thirds of the world's GDP and 85% of technology are produced by 40 mega-regions around the world.

These cities become pollution centers as soon as the weather gets hot and congestion is increasing. Infrastructures cannot cope. Productivity losses in traffic jams are huge. Moreover, few cities are able to radically transform their urban layout in order to create new traffic arteries (similar to what Baron Haussmann did in Paris in the 19th century).

In some emerging countries, it is possible to radically alter urbanized regions. This is what China did during the 2008 Olympic Games in Beijing. In other countries, it would lead to riots. Hence, some cities like London resort to congestion taxes or restrict vehicle use to alternate days. Yet, these are only makeshift measures. Congestion in our cities is the symptom of a deeper problem: we do not really know how to manage large cities today.

If we do not act quickly, even large cities in industrialized countries will become unmanageable. They will resemble the megalopolises of some developing countries, where even statisticians are unable to measure what is really happening.

Few municipalities have developed a blueprint to adapt to the growing needs of major cities. The sad reality is that we have few solutions for managing urban sprawl. Until this is done, people will continue to suffer from increasing losses in productivity.

A philosophy of waiting is appearing. In lines, in traffic, we check our emails, we read, we listen to music on our MP3 players. In short, we escape, but it is a poor expedient when mobility disappears, and congestion suffocates us ...

82

SHOULD WE GET UP AT 5 A.M.?

I am always impressed by the working habits of our treasured leaders. Almost all of them wake up between 2:30 a.m. and 5:00 a.m., run miles through town and through woods, then get through a colossal day's work at the office. I humbly admit that at 5:00 a.m. I am sound asleep ... Of course, I am not a leader ...

Americans today work on average 8 1/2 more hours per week than they did 30 years ago. Most adults sleep less and stress is on the rise. Who is to blame?

Technology follows us everywhere. The US company Good Technology, which specializes in mobile information, reckons that 80% of workers continue to work after they have left the office and 69% check their emails before going to bed. How many of us spend a day without checking – and answering – emails, texts and other messages?

The urgent has taken over from the important. In addition, a cult of relentless work has developed, as if working "more" necessarily means working "better."

It is a case of who gets to the office first and who leaves last. I must confess that I am as guilty as anyone else; often, in the past, I have woken up at 2:30 a.m. to work so that I could spend breakfast time with my young family. After that, though, I was a zombie for the rest of the day ...

Who is right? People are different: Napoleon and Margaret Thatcher only slept a few hours a night, whereas Winston Churchill enjoyed wallowing in his bath until late in the morning (some say with a bottle of champagne ...). It also depends on the job. A leader making a considerable number of decisions every day cannot avoid long hours.

The "creative worker," described by Peter Drucker, is not so lucky. Brilliant ideas do not always come during working hours. An idea can happen at any time; one must be prepared for it. The problem is that many leaders have agendas that are so full that every minute is occupied. As a result, they cannot take the time to stand back and look at the big picture.

Jack Welch, former president of General Electric, planned to have time every day to "look out the window." Others schedule fake appointments during the day to preserve some time for reflection. Companies often create vast amounts of inefficiency through the multiplication of emails, video conferences, voicemail and endless meetings ("death by PowerPoint") that lengthen the day but reduce productivity. This leads to the development of a culture of workaholics, whether at work, when traveling or, even worse, at home ...

Doing "more" does not necessarily mean doing "better." In fact, it is more intelligent to work less and better, than to work a lot without much thinking.

It may also be advisable to stop and take some time to ponder Suetonius' wisdom: "Festina Lente" ... make haste slowly.

83

ARE YOU IRREPLACEABLE?

"You are the most important resource of this company." In most companies, the CEO repeats this platitude at every staff meeting ... and everyone in the room chuckles because they know that it's not true. In times of hardship, employees have few illusions; they know they will be the first to bear the brunt of a crisis.

Since 2008, unemployment levels have reached high levels almost everywhere; in Europe, they are almost 12%. The International Labor Organization estimates that close to 200 million people are currently unemployed in the world. In addition, youth unemployment, i.e. those between 16 and 24 years old, is skyrocketing; it is over 50% in Spain and Greece ... Not great for people who are supposed to be irreplaceable ...

Despite the misconception, employees are indeed the most valuable part of an enterprise. After World War II, the American government laid off thousands of engineers who had been hired during the war effort. Companies such as Hewlett-Packard took advantage of this and hired them "en masse." Bill Hewlett and Dave Packard always said that hiring those engineers was one of the greatest opportunities of their business careers. Today, Google has one of the highest market capitalizations in the world. However, how much would Google be worth without its engineers and qualified employees?

The problem is that we do not know how to correctly value human resources in corporate accounting. We should be talking about human capital or assets. On the contrary, employees are accounted for as a cost. When an enterprise funds employee training, it appears in the books as an expenditure rather than an investment in the value of people and, therefore, the company. When the company fires an employee, it appears as if it has saved money, while in reality it is a "divestment." A cut in personnel is often considered a positive move by the stock exchange and share prices rise. This is absurd since in many cases the company, in fact, becomes poorer ...

I have often wondered what would have happened if human capital was recorded on the other side of the balance sheet, as an asset. In this case, parting with a trained employee with 20 years of expertise – who knows the business, technology, culture and clients – would be recorded as a loss of value. So why isn't this the case?

First, because employees do not belong to a company (contrary to what some CEO's think). Moreover, this wealth is nomadic; it leaves the company every evening and, during the night, the CEO hopes that it will come back the next day at 8 a.m. sharp.

How do you give an accounting value to "your company's most valuable assets" when, they wander the obscure streets of your city at night? Historically, this was why employees were paid on a weekly, then a monthly basis beginning at the end of the first month of employment; it was to make sure they came back.

Even if people are not accounted for adequately on the balance sheet, they are indeed the most valuable part of an enterprise. In that sense, we are all irreplaceable. Companies that understand the true value of their employees, enjoy enduring success in the long term. And leaders, who care about their employees, attract the best talent.

84

HOW TO REINVENT ONESELF?

The business world changes quickly, but what about us? As we saw earlier (*see Question 49: Why do large companies disappear?*), the average life expectancy of a company barely exceeds 40 years. Since 1955, *Fortune* magazine has published a list of America's biggest corporations. Less than 15% have survived throughout this period. During the past 20 years, 50% of them have disappeared from the list; they had been downsized, bought out, merged or gone bankrupt. For the first time, career life is exceeding the life expectancy of many organizations. At this rate, we can expect several jobs during our professional life; therefore, we should reinvent ourselves regularly.

According to Leo Tolstoy, "Everyone thinks of changing the world, but no one thinks of changing himself." But how can this be done? In fact, it is easier when things go wrong. You don't need great powers of persuasion to convince an employee to change when results are absent.

It becomes more complicated when performance is average. Why change a model that works, more or less? People prefer to wait until a crisis occurs. Peter Drucker summarized it this way, "A lot of managers have already retired at work." To make people change before a crisis strikes is a hard task.

Nothing is more exciting and difficult than reinventing oneself when success is still theirs. Success can be perilous. Picasso summarized it this way: "Success is dangerous – we have a tendency to copy ourselves – it's worse than copying others; it leads to sterility." Enterprises and people are always hostages of their history and above all of their past success. When a procedure works, we obviously develop a tendency to repeat it ad infinitum. If it works, do not change it! Until it is too late.

An automobile executive from Detroit told me in the 1980s, "Americans will never buy a small Japanese car – I have been in this business 30 years – I know!" In 1997, the Toyota Camry became the best-selling car in the United States – and stayed there for 11 years. "I know ...?"

This is what I call the pyramid syndrome. With success, little by little, we become isolated, similar to being at the summit of a pyramid; it is impossible to move upward, forward, backward or sideways. Instead, there are two choices: develop sclerosis at the top or go back down and climb another pyramid. By coming down, you are also reinventing yourself. It is sometimes difficult to do, but it provides an indispensable foundation for new and even greater success.

Many people do not realize that they have real value for the organizations they work for, but less value for other organizations. This is what often happens in large companies; people enjoy narrowly focused, specialized jobs that have less value elsewhere. It is thus necessary to keep in mind what you are worth outside of the company. Focusing on one's market value and employability should remain a priority in your career plan, even if you do not intend to change jobs immediately (*see Question 85: Do you have market value?*).

Reinvention is always a matter of courage, lucidity and imagination. It is first and foremost about picturing yourself tomorrow. If tomorrow is going to be different from today, so should you.

85

DO YOU HAVE MARKET VALUE?

It may seem inappropriate to raise the issue of people's market value as if they were slaves for sale on the public square. However, it exists. For example, salaries are a reflection of the value we hold in the economic world.

One of the great problems of employment is that too many people mistake their value inside an enterprise with their value on the job market. If people do not regularly monitor their market value, they incur a greater risk of not finding another similar position if their company restructures and they lose their job.

It was in response to this problem that I once had a brilliant idea ... that did not work. The objective was to make employees more aware of their market value beyond the work and responsibilities they held in the company.

Indeed, too many large corporations "disconnect" their employees from economic reality and from the daily work environment of the average employee. They are well paid; they work in modern offices and they have assistance for many things in life, such as travel, children's education and moving. Consequently, they live in a kind of "cocoon" created by the enterprise to ensure their loyalty.

The assumption was that an employee, who is disconnected from the outside world, also becomes more vulnerable in times of change. The theory was that, in such cases, employees would not only be confronted with the economic consequences of job loss but also with significant psychological trauma. Companies are often perceived by employees as a second family and they contribute significantly to personal identity. Moreover, we had noticed that employees conscious of this vulnerability became more hostile towards risk-taking. They were well aware of all they could lose, and feared that they would not be able to compensate for that loss. In contrast, employees who knew their market value were more likely to take risks because they knew that they had alternatives elsewhere.

The idea was to ask employees to regularly evaluate not only their contribution to the company but also their market value just in case they ran into problems. In order to do so, they had to check whether their internal competencies were also recognized externally. They also had to evaluate whether their work experience and their aptitudes could have value in another company. They were offered the help of a consultant and an outsourcing agency. Of course, the approach was purely theoretical but it did not work out ...

"Come on, tell us the truth; you want to get rid of us, don't you?" As is often the case in economics, the law of unintended consequences was at work. Instead of helping people feel more secure in their work, by showing them that they also had a market value, it destabilized everybody.

Despite this failure, there is no doubt that an employee with real market value is always more flexible and more of a risk taker than someone who just looks inward. When a company needs to restructure, it is easier to redeploy employees who have a market value than to deal with those who run the risk of becoming assisted by the social system.

Though this brilliant idea did not work and vanished into oblivion, I cannot help feeling that we were on to something ...

86

DO YOU REALLY NEED AN OFFICE?

In his book *The Age of Unreason*, published in 1991, Charles Handy, one of the most prolific authors on the transformation of work, wrote, "In 10 years' time more than half of the jobs will not be jobs in the traditional definition of the word. People with a full-time job or working inside an enterprise will be the new minority." Although his prediction has not fully materialized, he recognized the trend early. People increasingly work for a company without "being part of it." The Aberdeen Group estimates that approximately 26% of company employees are "contingent." What does this imply?

The increase in part-time contracts, freelance work and even tele-working has led to the development of a circle of collaborators who work "with" a company, but are not "inside" of it. This flexibility is a huge advantage for the company, but the psychological impact on employees is significant. Is it possible to develop a sense of belonging and dedication without being inside a company's premises and having an office?

The relationship with one's office is particularly complex because it affects not only the work environment but also the mindset of col-laborators. An office is often perceived as a "fortress." In order to favor communication, open-concept offices have proliferated notably in large companies. Everyone is part of the same workspace and offices are only separated by low partitions to guarantee minimum privacy. Only the conference or meeting rooms remain closed.

Michael Bloomberg, who founded the eponymous financial ser-vices company and later became mayor of New York, placed his desk in the center of an open-space office surrounded by other desks. He is also said to have discouraged the use of elevators in order to encourage people to meet in the stairway.

Oticon, a company that produces hearing aids in Denmark, has gone one step further and pioneered an approach called "hoteling." Having noticed that offices were often empty during the week because collaborators traveled, the company invented an office reservation system (hence the name). Each collaborator could reserve a working space with standard equipment and use it for a fixed period. All they had to do was collect a trolley at the reception with all of their office and personal belongings. And they could begin their day.

In the United States, Sam Walton, founder of Walmart, the largest supermarket chain in the world, insisted that the offices of his directors remain as "Spartan" as possible. The objective was to make sure that managers spent most of their time "outside" their office visiting clients and supermarkets. The French Newspaper *Le Monde* remains famous for organizing its editorial meetings "standing up," which drastically reduced the length of discussions ...

In spite of all these innovations, the old perceptions about work in the office die hard; a "real" job is still associated with an enterprise, a building, a full-time workload and a title: "Your husband works from home? Hmm, he must not have a real job then?"

87

HOW SHOULD YOU DRESS AT WORK?

Although it is said that you cannot judge people by the way they dress, things are different in companies. The dress code is more complex and more important than first meets the eye. Job consultants say that you should dress for the position you seek. In a job interview, a candidate's dress indicates the expectation he has of the company and the professional image he wants to project. Attire is part of the branding of a company and of a person.

The business world was traditionally the suit and tie. Some companies even went as far as suggesting typical colors: white shirt, dark blue suit, red tie, black shoes and so forth. This was the objective of Thomas J. Watson, Sr., the founder of IBM, who was also known for never taking off his jacket, even on the hottest day. The idea was to reinforce the sense of belonging and project a consistent image to customers. As Voltaire noticed, "Dress changes manners."

In Asia, enterprises sometimes go further; the uniform is mandatory. I remember, some years ago, visiting Sony's headquarters in Tokyo. Everyone wore identical suits and the only way to distinguish the president (Akio Morita at the time) from his colleagues was the badge on his jacket (I exaggerate slightly ...).

Today, things are different. Oscar Wilde thought one could never be "overdressed [...]" Yet, California has a different take on the matter. There, it is the "suit and tie" that are unfashionable. Reverse snobbery favors a casual approach in the workplace: faded t-shirts, torn jeans and sandals.

The aim is to look "cool," just like the tech gurus that prompted the fortunes of Silicon Valley. It is also a message from entrepreneurs to the younger generation that has been the early adopter of such innovations: we are like you ... Who started this trend? Steve Jobs, perhaps? In any case, this new dress code has become the norm, and not only in California. Sometimes, managers of more traditional businesses explore this new style and end up looking a bit weird!

Today's top fashion statement is the hoody, made famous by Mark Zuckerberg, the founder of Facebook. It has become the symbol of an entire generation that is a bit anti-establishment and eager for differentiation. As this new generation represents potential customers and voters, everyone is adopting the casual look; from managers to politicians who want to show that they are "cool." Within certain limits, of course. When visiting Facebook, Barack Obama boasted he was the only man who could prompt Mark Zuckerberg to wear a tie ...

Inside "traditional" companies, the situation is more complicated. Even in the most "right-minded" companies, conferences and meetings off-site can take place without a tie. Some companies have also tried to make Friday an informal day, allowing a more relaxed dress code unless there is a meeting with a client. More surprisingly, studies have shown that the economic situation also influences employees' dress codes: in times of crisis or uncertainty, formal wear reappears ...

The dress code reflects changing values. In companies, the older generation in a suit and tie often meets the middle-aged one, wearing a jacket and open-collar, and then the younger one in its now famous hoodie. Even women have greater freedom in what they choose to wear at the office: the standard little black dress of former times is disappearing.

Thus, the way you dress in a company or in a given situation is first a matter of judgment. Keep in mind the advice of the 17th century British clergyman Thomas Fuller: "Good clothes open all doors."

88

MAKING A SPEECH OR
SPEAKING TO PEOPLE?

Delivering a good speech is quite easy." I was listening attentively to former British Prime Minister Edward Heath, the man who brought Great Britain into Europe in 1973. He was probably the most gifted speaker I have ever met; he was able to captivate an audience without notes. A product of the British "debating societies" that acquainted students with the art of public speaking and dialectics. I asked him the secret of this oratory skill. He said, "In fact you should not deliver speeches, you should talk to people." That is all ...

Simple and true ... In Shakespeare's Henry IV, Falstaff advises the king that to be popular with his subjects he must "enter their world." If "true eloquence disregards eloquence," as Blaise Pascal wrote, it only becomes authentic if the listener feels a particular bond with the speaker and indeed enters his world. This is called empathy. Without it, the most exciting speeches are nothing but an exercise in empty style, which navigates between pretentiousness and pedantry.

It is also necessary to take one's time. One day, during a press conference, Raymond Barre – another prime minister, French this time – whispered in my ear, "Garelli, what should I say?" I quickly scribbled an answer. Raymond Barre quietly took the piece of paper and, before reading, corrected the French accents I did not have time to add. All the while, the room waited. He was in charge and setting the tempo. If a speech is rushed, the audience will also expect it to be over soon.

The words must be simple. No use in making it complicated. The first time I appeared on CNN, the presenter gave me the following instructions, a few minutes before going on air, "Remember, you are speaking to people who are 12 years old!" I was shocked. Yet, it is possible to say important things simply.

Stress is natural, even necessary. Hans Selye, a Hungarian professor and a pioneer on the subject, described it like this: "Stress is like salt in a soup, if there isn't any it is tasteless; if there is too much, it is inedible." He distinguished between the positive "eu-stress" and the negative "dis-stress."

What is important, therefore, is to transform stress into stimulus and not inhibition. When facing people, one can make many errors, which will be forgiven if they feel you are really "speaking" to them.

Helmut Schmidt, a former German chancellor, could speak brilliantly about politics and economics while being passionate about modern art and music. The chancellery in Bonn had become a museum during his terms in office and he had recorded piano concertos by J.S. Bach. He knew how to switch from one field to the other with equal ease. A good speaker is also a well-read person with a broader perspective.

And, of course, the last word should stir a lasting emotion. How many times have I heard people praise such and such a speaker? But when asked, "What did he say?" and the answer is, "I cannot remember but it was fantastic," this is not very useful.

French writer Sacha Guitry liked to say, "The silence after a Mozart concerto is also Mozart." Good speeches, like good music, should prompt people to think and have a long-lasting impact – quite rare ...

89

DOES SUCCESS HAVE ITS OWN RULES?

It would be easy to write a book of recipes about how to become successful. American authors have become experts in this domain. The theory of competitiveness also brings a certain number of answers. My students often ask for them. Here are a few:

Find your uniqueness. Being good is not enough; we must be different. We each have a talent that distinguishes us from others; discovering it is the aim. For some, it is conceptual intelligence, for others manual intelligence. Some have a talent for action, others for reflection. Every strategy is an exercise in differentiation. The same goes for individuals.

Compare yourself. If we run 100 meters in 15 seconds and we are able to reduce this time to 13 seconds, we will be eminently satisfied with ourselves. Yet such a performance would place us last at the Olympic Games. What matters is not only measuring one's performance but also comparing it to others. It can be highly frustrating. One can improve, but perhaps not as much as others improve; thus, competitiveness is lost.

Maximize your advantage. Of course, we all want to do something interesting. But there exists a fundamental principle in economics: if a lot of people have the same competencies and little differentiation, they won't have access to high salaries. Economic success depends upon the capacity to differentiate yourself from others. The same goes for enterprises. Those in packed sectors, like food distribution, do not have high-profit margins. In contrast, those that are more unique in their domain generate high levels of profitability, e.g. Google and Microsoft.

Execute flawlessly. The capacity to transform an idea into results is essential for competitiveness success. It is good to have dreams, but dreams must also have deadlines. The majority of enterprises do not fail because they have a bad strategy; they fail because of poor implementation.

Persist. As Thomas Edison once said, "Genius is 1% inspiration and 99% perspiration." Today, successes may be reached more rapidly than in the past, thanks, for example, to the Internet. However, 30-year-old billionaires are the exception. Hard work and perseverance remain the rule.

Stay positive. Practically nobody succeeds on the first attempt. The capacity to react and be in good spirits is a fundamental element of success and competitiveness. Politicians have a lot to teach us in this field. President Ronald Reagan liked to call himself the "Teflon President."

And Winston Churchill summarized it all perfectly as follows: "Success consists of going from failure to failure without loss of enthusiasm!"

90

CAN ONE BE OVEREDUCATED?

In the words of Oscar Wilde: "You can never be overdressed or over-educated." Brilliant, but is it still true today? We still overdress, compared to our children, but surprisingly, it is actually possible to be overeducated today.

South Korea regularly comes first in the rankings of countries with the best education systems according to the OECD PISA study. Education has become a national obsession there. Yet, every year more than 50,000 university graduates cannot find a job. On the other hand, there are not enough candidates for the more than 30,000 jobs offered to people with secondary school qualifications. The Samsung Economic Research Institute reckons that more than 40% of university graduates are "overeducated."

In Europe, the educational top rank often goes to Finland. The country welcomes numerous delegations who seek to learn from the Finnish "miracle." There is no doubt that the system is excellent, and yet ... The unemployment rate of young people between 16 and 24 exceeds 20% – three times higher than that of Switzerland. Like South Korea, Finland overeducates its young people who ultimately cannot, or do not want to, find work. Why?

It comes from our obsession with university education. In the OECD, 56% of young people aged 18 and above who graduate from secondary school go to university. In South Korea and Finland, the figure is more than 90%. This ambition is understandable. Who does not want their children to graduate from university? Then, there is the financial impact; in Great Britain, a university graduate earns 66% more than someone who holds a baccalaureate (or a secondary school diploma) does. In countries where apprenticeships are well developed, unemployment among young people is at its lowest: 6.1% in Switzerland and 8.1% in Germany.

At university, one acquires knowledge; in the apprenticeship system, one learns a trade. It is much more interesting for young scholars to study Steve Jobs' strategies or Warren Buffet's approach to finance, than Super Mario's plumbing techniques.

However, after university none of the graduates will be involved in strategy for a number of years. Add a little advanced math and our young elite believe they are at the pinnacle of knowledge. But the fall will be harder because they still have not mastered the "know-how."

Of course, one should never forget that an important percentage of the population, even in industrialized countries, suffers from functional illiteracy (an inability to read correctly, to write and to understand simple text). Yet a good education requires a two-pronged approach. Alongside the scholarly system that teaches some how to master "a science," there must be an apprenticeship system that teaches others how to master "a profession."

Both roads must lead to the same level of respect and success in society. Otherwise young academics will continue to be "underemployed" and young apprentices" undervalued." A tremendous waste for everybody!

91

ARE WE HONEST?

Security, or rather the sense of insecurity, has a major impact on how enterprises treat its clients. Should customers be considered potential crooks, or are the majority of clients honest? Tough question ...

Dishonesty is clearly perceived differently depending on where you live. According to the IMD report on world competitiveness, countries that have the greatest sense of personal security, private property and goods protection are Finland, Denmark, Norway, Canada and Switzerland. It is more or less the same for the absence of corruption. At the bottom of the list are the Latin American countries, Ukraine and Romania.

These statistics seem to validate the famous "wallet test." You find a wallet on the street containing a few banknotes. You are alone, nobody sees you, but the owner's address is inside. What do you do? In Scandinavian countries, more than 90% of wallets are returned either to the owner or to the police. In Switzerland, three-quarters are returned. In some Latin American countries, less than 30% are returned.

Faced with this situation, companies must determine whether clients are *à priori* honest or not. For instance, many of us have experienced the fraudulent use of our credit cards. The hardest hit countries in the world are Mexico, the United States and India. However, according to the European Central Bank, the amount of illicit operations in Europe does not exceed 0.03% of all transactions. On a global level, credit card fraud does not exceed 0.1% of transactions.

And in shops? Today, shoplifting represents between 1% and 1.5% of a supermarket's turnover. It is a little higher for smaller shops that are not as well equipped with security measures.

These figures show that the vast majority of clients are honest (98%). However, are they always treated accordingly? Many stores continue to be suspicious of customers who stroll along the aisles without any precise idea of what they want to buy.

Many companies balk at exchanging defective products because they suspect dishonesty. Such attitudes have profoundly harmed the reputations of numerous businesses and alienated clients – so much so that some companies have decided to take a chance on honesty.

In France, Darty advertises and guarantees the lowest prices, and pays the difference to customers if they can find the product for less elsewhere. In the United States, Walmart went one step further: it was one of the first enterprises to establish a "satisfaction or your money back" policy. Even if your purchase was a mistake, your money will be reimbursed. The objective is customer satisfaction and trust....

It would appear that we are honest after all. Nevertheless, it is sometimes difficult to convince certain companies. It implies that better employee training and especially a change in mindset are required.

92

ARE YOU HAPPY?

In 1972, Bhutan created an index assessing its population's happiness, the so-called Gross National Happiness Index. The concept makes sense since the objective of any nation's policy is to advance its prosperity and, consequently, to increase a population's sense of well-being and happiness. In fact, the idea was so good that such indexes became common.

In 2013, the *Economist Intelligence Unit* published an index of the best places to be born. Switzerland came first followed by Australia, Norway, Sweden and Denmark. More recently, three organizations (the International Youth Foundation, the Center for Strategic and International Studies and the Hilton Corporation) have tried to evaluate where young people were happiest. It appears to be Australia, then Sweden, South Korea, the United Kingdom and Germany.

Prosperity is a concept that applies to a community of people, such as a nation, whereas happiness remains a very individual feeling. The "pursuit of happiness" appears in the declaration of independence of the United States, but it has remained a relatively unique occurrence. Generally, well-being or happiness is a rather personal sentiment, which is difficult to analyze from an economic point of view.

Moreover, some people seem to have a natural inclination for happiness. Aristotle, in his "Nicomachean Ethics," believed that happiness was the objective (telos) of life. He stressed that some people were born with a natural inclination for happiness and that only the practice of philosophy and virtue could increase it. Genetics has reinforced this point of view 2000 years later. Oxytocin, a hormone, and serotonin, a neurotransmitter, are inherited in our genome. They are critical for triggering happiness and treating depression. It seems that certain practices, such as meditation, can also increase their presence in our body. A positive attitude also helps.

What about material success? Angus Deaton, the winner of the 2015 Nobel prize in economics, believes that happiness is correlated to income, but only up to $75,000 a year. After this threshold, more qualitative aspects of life become predominant. Lee Kwan Yew, the late prime minister of Singapore, advised that people should experience the benefits of a country's economic success in everyday life. He, therefore, maintained that the population should enjoy visible improvements in hospitals, schools, roads, public transport and housing because economic growth should translate into well-being for everyone.

The same goes for companies. Bill Hewlett, one of the founders of Hewlett-Packard, used to say, "If you give your employees a good working environment, they will naturally work well." Companies where employees are "happy" are those where motivation and innovation are the highest. *Fortune* regularly ranks the most attractive enterprises to work for; unsurprisingly, Google regularly tops the list.

The limit of rankings and national policies are that they only focus on the external impact on happiness. South Korea has the same GDP per capita as Greece but a rate of suicide (28.9 per 100,000) which is almost nine times higher. Japan, which is the world's third-largest economy, has the highest rate of suicide in advanced nations (18.5 per 100,000). Prosperity and well-being matter for happiness, but there is more to it. Money does not make people happy, but the absence of it can make anyone quite unhappy …

Happiness is thus an elusive concept. It is the result of policies that lead to prosperity and of visions that foster hope. And the more prosperity is in peril, the more hope matters for happiness. Former British Prime Minister Edward Heath once told me, "If we cannot succeed in regularly giving people hope, then we have failed in our mission." Unfortunately, in periods of crisis, leaders regularly tend to forget this …

93

WERE YOU BORN AT THE WRONG TIME?

If you are between 40 and 50 years old today, you may believe the golden age was a few decades ago.

Back then, at a similar age, our children were grown and had left home. Our parents were still young enough to take care of themselves. It was a carefree time of convertible cars, yachting and travels. Today, the roaring forties roar somewhat less. For the first time, 40- to 50-year-olds face a four-generation economy. They have to deal with aging grandparents, parents, children who refuse to grow-up and their own lives.

In Great Britain, more than 3 million young people between 20 and 34 years old still live with their parents. In crisis-hit southern Europe, young people increasingly take refuge with their parents. Sometimes, even if they leave, they end up coming back ... The "boomerang" generation is a new feature everywhere. There is no longer a stigma associated with living at home with your parents.

Demographics is perhaps to blame. Germany's Max Planck Institute has shown that a person living in 1800 had an average lifespan closer to that of a caveman 20,000 years ago: 32 to 35 years. Since then, progress in medicine has increased the average life expectancy to above 82 years in most advanced economies. Today, life expectancy is increasing by around five hours every day. However, it also implies that there will be an increase in retirement and health care cost.

Each generation is marked by its own distinct value system. The difference today is that a generation does not replace another but adds to the others. The result is something of a mess.

For enterprises, the question is no longer about how to adapt to the values of new generations, but rather how to ensure that these new values are compatible with those from one or two generations earlier. How to ensure that those who come to the office in a suit and tie can live side by side with those who consider a pair of jeans to be their Sunday best (*see Question 87: How should you dress at work?*).

Work increases the pressure. The "middle" generation feels it needs to succeed ever faster. According to Egon Zehnder (the recruitment company), the number of CEOs in their forties has doubled to 40% in 15 years. Young millionaires in their thirties are becoming more common. And to top it off, young executives want to have children and a family life.

Nowadays, well-off parents have their children after 30, when their careers are taking off. This implies a high level of work and family organization, juggling the day-to-day with a daunting agenda. Not everybody is a Marissa Meyer, who became the head of Yahoo at 37, while pregnant ...

If our societies have become intergenerational and multicultural, so have our enterprises. This is where the 40- to 50-year-old generation has a fundamental role to play. It is the link between the past and the future and it understands the aspirations of both its younger and older colleagues.

Work has thus become the meeting point of people who have increasingly different backgrounds, life objectives and value systems. The new challenge for corporate culture is to ensure that this cross-section of people cohabits happily – not easy ...

94

ARE YOU HOOKED ON DIGITAL?

Do a test: turn off your telephone, do not look at your computer, surf the Internet or check your emails and see how long you can last. If, after a few hours, you start to feel edgy, you become worried, nervous, anxious, then there is no doubt – you are hooked on the digital world. This disease is not serious, but it is an addiction that affects a large part of the population.

Being connected 24 hours a day creates stress. Any employee who leaves for a business trip or holiday is terrified at the thought of messages piling up on his computer. Instead of waiting until his return, he surreptitiously checks his messages in a taxi or on the beach and then he gets stressed again. Despite anti-spam software, we get hundreds of emails every day, which the sender believes are very important.

In 2011, Volkswagen initiated a policy to protect employees. The company stopped redirecting emails to employees' mobile phones outside of working hours. In more and more companies today, managers are encouraged not to send emails to their colleagues during weekends or holidays. In this case, the employee has a right not to answer immediately.

It is becoming popular to leave an email notification saying that one is absent. However, employees worry that they will appear lazy or uninterested in their work if they do not respond. In practice, we are expected to answer emails within 24 hours, whether one is traveling, sick, on holidays or not. Another German company, Daimler, tried a new "mail on holiday" notification system. It informs the sender that the message was not distributed to the recipient because of holidays and it provides an alternative contact person.

Individuals can also address the issue through discipline, i.e. only read emails during well-defined time slots to avoid being disrupted during work. It is also recommended that you stop reading emails late in evening to avoid anxiety and insomnia. The email issue extends to voice and video messages; in this case, it is impossible to rush things:

you have to listen to three minutes of message before hearing, "This was merely for your information." Social networks add to the amount of shared information; WhatsApp and SMS now account for almost 50 billion messages each day ...

The digital world is fascinating but also intrusive, especially at home. Americans spend on average 34 hours a week watching TV (3.5 hours daily for children between 2 and 11). Internet surfing on a PC or smartphone adds 5 hours per week. In the US, Americans collectively check their phone 8 billion times each day. On average, people look at their phone 46 times per day! Social media also increases the pressure; in China, subscribers to WeChat spend 20 hours a month on messages.

Can we escape from the digital world? California, always a step ahead, has begun offering "digital detox camps." Participants leave their smartphones in the cloakroom and they are not allowed to check their messages on the sly. They learn to live again with the carelessness of the old days when nobody knew where they were, what they were up to and what they looked like at 10:24 a.m. yesterday.

It has even been suggested that the US create a national day of "disconnection," in order to "reconnect" with life. Not a bad idea ...

95

WILL YOU AGE ALONE?

As life expectancy increases, the impact on our quality of life in old age remains uncertain. In developed countries, people live, on average, more than 82 years. Living longer is good news. In Europe, the median age has risen from 29 years in 1950 to 40 today. In North America, it has increased from 30 to 37 and in Asia from 22 to 29.

It is no longer unusual to become a centenarian. Currently, Japan has 34 centenarians per 100,000 people, followed by Italy and France with 27, Thailand and Spain with 26, Canada, the United Kingdom and Germany with 22.

Becoming a centenarian is still considered to be an unusual achievement in many countries. In the United Kingdom, the Queen sends a message of congratulations, the president of the United States does the same. In Japan, they receive a certificate from the prime minister; in Sweden, a telegram from the King and Queen is sent; and in Ireland, a prize of €2,500 is awarded. Each country has its priorities. Honoring centenarians may become a full-time job for heads of state.

An aging population is the result of better medical care, but also a drop in fertility. Today, the replacement rate of populations – which is 2.1 births per family – is not reached by most countries in North America or Europe. In Asia, there is more of a contrast: the birth rates in China, Japan, Korea, and Thailand are lower than 2.1, whereas the population in India, Indonesia and the Philippines continues to grow. In 2050, seniors over 60 around the world will be more numerous than children under 15.

The consequences for older citizens will be many: extended working years, insecure pension benefits and increased medical expenses. But it is not all bad news. It is estimated that those who are 55 years old and over are now responsible for approximately 55% of consumption spending in advanced economies. "Wealth and health" has become the new priority as the "silver generation" expands.

A more disturbing aspect of this revolution is that more people will live alone in their old age. In Europe, like in the US, approximately 75% of people over 60 live independently. They are not in an assisted environment, nor are they living with their children or in a nursing home. This figure is below 30% in Asia. In traditional Asian culture, influenced by Confucianism, grandparents stay at home; they are cared for by their children and in return, they take care of the grand-children. This approach fulfills not only a cultural function but also responds to an economic necessity. It is the only way to take care of aging people when the pension system is not yet adequately funded, as is often the case in emerging economies.

In Europe and the US, children are often eager to leave home early to start their own family. Aging parents then pursue their existence on their own until they have to enter a nursing home or a medicalized institution. Modern technologies have made it possible for aging people to remain at home longer; their health can be monitored remotely from a doctor's office or from a hospital.

Of course, this is progress. Unfortunately, it also increases the isolation of elderly people in our society. Remote health monitoring through connected medical devices also limits the essential interaction of older people with other human beings. A deep feeling of loneliness can take hold. Why live longer, if the price to pay is an increased feeling of remoteness and isolation? For future generations of old people, advances in science and technology are good and necessary. However, the emotional and human consequences of getting older must also be addressed. One does not go without the other.

96

IS DIVORCE A GOOD BUSINESS?

It obviously depends on whom you are married to. If you wed a Russian oligarch who distributes banknotes like confetti, or a rich, off-the-wall, Californian heiress, divorce may effectively be a good deal. Nevertheless, for the majority of the population divorce primarily translates into economic impoverishment.

The divorce rate in the United States is 53%, and in Europe, the average is 44%. There are considerable differences among countries, ranging from 71% in Belgium to 15% in Ireland (because of the influence of the Catholic Church). Religious aspects do not explain everything. The divorce rate is 68% in Portugal and 65% in Spain, yet only 25% in Italy. Nowadays, only the Philippines bans divorce. Failure rates get worse if repeated. American statistics show that the divorce rates for a second marriage are 67% and 73% for the third. In other words, the more you try, the less you succeed. This does not seem to discourage some people ...

For many, impoverishment from a broken marriage is simply the result of the application of a fundamental principle of business: economies of scale. To make it simple, size and the pooling of resources and revenues leads to a reduction in the cost per unit. This means that when a family lives in the same apartment, cooks in the same kitchen, watches the same TV or uses the same washing machine, it develops greater economic efficiency than if each member of the family lived individually. After the divorce, the broken family becomes two smaller groups. Consequently, the cost per "family unit" increases to preserve the same standard of living.

In addition, revenues are shared less efficiently (for example, through the alimony system). Legal expenses must also be added, including attorneys who can make the operation especially expensive. There are 1.2 million attorneys in the US, of which a number specialize only in divorce. Americans like to say that when an attorney lives alone in a small town, he drives a cheap car but as soon as a second attorney arrives, both soon drive expensive cars.

From an economic point of view, divorce does not have only negative effects. In many countries, it has contributed to the development of real estate, by multiplying the amount of housing necessary.

In countries with a high divorce rate, a growing proportion of women take jobs, often through necessity, rather than choice. However, statistics have more difficulty in evaluating the impact of those undeclared couples who "split up," or of recomposed families that do not necessarily have legal status.

So why do people divorce? Answers are many and varied. Some say because of evolving attitudes. This is not convincing because yesterday's attitudes were as dissolute as today's, except that divorce was not an option (the bourgeois stayed married, but had a mistress ...).

Others argue that the separation of state and Church has led to a "decriminalization" of divorce. Put simply, it does not lead to hell anymore ...

Finally, there is the anthropological explanation: we, Homo sapiens, had a life expectancy of 30 to 35 years and did not spend more than 20 years with the same companion. Nowadays, as the life expectancy of both exceeds 80 years, it is much harder and more difficult to stay together for a longer period. This may explain the mid-life crisis ...

97

IS THERE A FUTURE
FOR HANDWRITING?

One of the consequences of computers, tablets and smartphones is that handwriting is disappearing. Postal traffic has been directly affected. The number of letters distributed is dropping regularly by between 2% and 5% per year and they are often being replaced by emails, texts or mobile applications. What will happen to good old handwritten messages?

Handwriting fulfills three functions: to communicate, archive and authenticate. Voltaire is famous for his correspondence – over 20,000 referenced letters! Mesopotamia invented cuneiform script mainly for the accounting of food storage and commercial transactions. Today, contracts are mainly signed in writing. Soon all of these functions will be done electronically, including storage of information by way of cloud technology.

Despite these developments, handwriting survives. Many enterprises continue to produce writing "instruments"; there are over 40 pen makers and more than 170 different brands of pencils worldwide! One of the oldest enterprises is Germany's Faber Castel, founded in 1761. Caran d'Ache in Switzerland dates from 1915. There is obviously a market for things handwritten. What is it?

Handwriting has become a luxury. For this reason, pencils or pens have often become luxury objects themselves. Handwriting is part of an intimate private sphere. A message of congratulations, of love or condolences, is written by hand. Christmas and New Year cards are – or should be – written and signed by hand. They underline a sense of belonging to the most intimate circle of contacts – the famous 150 identified by the anthropologist Robin Dunbar (*see Question 78: How many friends do you need?*). This is true in Western culture. In the East, handwriting has an additional artistic value – calligraphy.

In the year 353, the famous calligrapher Wang Xizhi invited 42 well-read guests to a party celebrating spring. Each had to sit close to a stream on which cups of wine were floating. When one of cups of wine drifted near a guest, he had to drink it and write a poem. At daybreak, Wang Xizhi was invited to write a preface as a remembrance – "Poems composed at the Orchid Pavilion" (Lantingji Xu).

His writing was so beautiful that legend has it that Wang Xizhi tried to copy it more than 100 times during his lifetime, without ever attaining the excellence of the original. Two centuries later, Emperor Li Shimin (Taizhong), founder of the illustrious Tang dynasty, expressed the desire to be buried with this perfect calligraphy, so he had it stolen.

Calligraphy, which can sometimes be compared to the illuminated manuscripts of the Middle Ages, may be the future of handwriting. It will probably remain the ultimate expression of personal thought, and the highest regard we can give to someone, to an idea or to oneself.

However, what will remain of the rest? Of all that has been transmitted, electronically or in the form of images? There may be a great void ...

98

WILL PAPER DISAPPEAR?

Today, magazines, newspapers and booksellers face the same issue: how to confront the declining use of paper. Tablets, e-book readers, and smartphones have altered the way we access information. Today global digital content is estimated to be close to 9 zettabytes. It would take 2,200 billion DVDs to make a backup. In short, it is a lot of information ... What will become of paper?

The disappearance of paper is nothing new. The arrival of the "paperless" office 20 years ago was supposed to change the way we worked forever. Though computers, telephones and scanners have transformed life in the office, we continue to produce considerable amounts of paper. The industry leader, Hewlett-Packard sells around $25 billion worth of printers each year ...

Paper is more than just a support for information. It also creates a psychological and emotional relationship with its user. New technologies have generated new approaches to information. Even smartphones are not named appropriately. They are used less as telephones and increasingly as mobile computers. For example, the Samsung Galaxy S5 has 2.5 million times more processing power than the computer that flew Apollo 11! In addition, smartphone market penetration in the population is impressive: 90% in the United Arab Emirates, 87% in Singapore and Saudi Arabia, 83% in Korea and in 79% in Norway in 2015.

What is this computing power used for? In most cases to watch movies or videos (in 2015, Netflix accounted for 37% of Internet bandwidth use in the US), to send messages and to manage one's life on social networks. In short to do all sorts of things that a newspaper or a book cannot do. So, what is left for paper?

During the great debate on the paperless office, scholars had already asked the question: is paper just paper, or is there something more? Psychological studies showed that when a person considered a piece of information important and wanted to "own" it, they would print it. It appears that digital information, seen on a screen, does not provide the same sense of "possession" as identical information on paper. Digital information belongs to everyone while a paper document is more personal, even intimate. It can easily be shared, annotated and stored on a shelf.

The introduction of new information technologies did not replace previous mediums; it multiplied them. Radio did not kill newspapers; it added to them. Similarly, television did not eliminate radio and the Internet did not eradicate television ... Each innovation completes the previous one. However, as the span-of-attention for obtaining information remains the same for consumers, each new technology takes a piece of the existing market. Consequently, old technologies experience a drop in revenues.

Paper will preserve its attractiveness for valuable information, especially if it has emotional content, such as a novel or poetry. In short, if it requires quality time to read it. Paper will thus continue to prevail for information that readers want to access intellectually and physically, for example placing it on a bookshelf for future reference.

A new business model will probably emerge; during the week, digital information will be the rule, but during the weekend and during long holidays, paper, including traditional books, will reclaim their rights.

99

IS ART A GOOD INVESTMENT?

The popular myth of the lonely artist disparaged during life and dying in abject poverty is not necessarily the rule. Many of the most famous works of art were sponsored by the state (Parthenon), patrons of the arts (the Medici), art collectors (Emperor Qianlong) and sold by shrewd gallery owners (Ambroise Vollard for the Impressionists) and auction houses. Thus, money and art have always been intimately linked. Annual transactions in the global art market reached $55 billion in 2014 and the number of collectors worldwide exceeds 70 million.

It would appear that every year, prices reach new highs. The record was set by Paul Cézanne. In 2012, "The Card Player" was auctioned off to Qatar for $271 million. Pablo Picasso is also quite sought after; his painting "The Dream" was sold for $157 million in 2013. In May 2015, his "Femmes d'Alger" broke records at an auction at Christie's in New York: $179 million! If the list of top sales is long, there are also some heartening discoveries ...

In Great Britain, a Chinese vase from the Qianlong period (end of the 18th century) was sold at an auction for the astounding price of $70 million. It had been found in the attic of a modest family home in the suburbs of London. Nobody knows how it got there. Perhaps, it was a souvenir brought back by a British soldier, who took part in the sacking of the Summer Palace in Beijing in 1860. A soldier with excellent taste ...

Art also has an important economic value for the development and attractiveness of a country. In Italy, a study has shown that its cultural sector generates revenue equivalent to 9.3% of its GDP and creates nearly 3 million jobs. France remains the world's top tourist destination with 83 million visitors in 2014 that spend on average some $50 billion each year. Of course, France has beautiful scenery, but its cultural heritage is the main attraction for tourists. Many emerging economies also see art as an essential complement to their economic attractiveness. China, India, Brazil and the Gulf countries invest massively in exhibitions and cultural events.

A most interesting development is the internationalization of museums. The Guggenheim museum in New York has been a pioneer in the field. There are now Guggenheim museums in Venice, Bilbao and Abu Dhabi. The Louvre in Paris followed the same path. It has just signed a contract with Abu Dhabi for the opening of a "subsidiary" in the United Arab Emirates. Today, countries realize that their attractiveness is not solely perceived from an economic point of view. They must also be able to offer a cultural environment that attracts the best talent and their families.

Art is a superb vehicle for the image of a country. Generally, the "nouveaux riches" of emerging countries buy and repatriate the art of their country. This is what Russian oligarchs did when they raced to purchase the famous Fabergé eggs scattered around the world. In 2007, one such egg sold for $18 million!

The same goes for China; a painting by Wang Meng (1350) reached $65 million in 2011. Now a younger generation of artists has become a hit with the "nouveau riche": Zhang Xiaogang has already sold more than $44 million worth of paintings and Yue Minjun $30 million. Both are in their 50s ...

Is art a good investment? Probably! However, never buy a work of art that you love ... because if you do, you will grow attached to it and will never sell it. And art will no longer be an investment, but a life-long passion!

100

WHY NOT?

Jean-Baptiste Charcot was an exceptional French explorer. He led many explorations to the North Pole and Antarctica, where a stretch of land bears his name. He died in 1936 when, returning from an expedition, his ship sank off the coast of Iceland. France gave him a state funeral. His frame of mind was reflected in the name he gave to several of his boats, "Le Pourquoi Pas?" – "Why not?"

This "Why not?" mindset is what we need today, in companies and nations. Robert Kennedy, quoting George Bernard Shaw, summarized it well, "Some men see things as they are and say, why; I dream things that never were and say, why not?"

Innovations are often blocked by "wise men" who look down upon everything with universal skepticism. However, every great success has, at its origin, something that would not have resisted logical analysis.

Who would have thought that one could be successful selling flights for less than $100? Who would have guessed that customers would rush to buy furniture that they had to carry home and build themselves? Who would have bet on the success of restaurants where clients would have to pick-up their meal at a counter and eat it with their fingers? Who, finally, would have believed that millions of people would want to share their private lives and their family photographs online with millions of unknown web surfers? EasyJet, IKEA, McDonalds and Facebook have done it. They dared to think the unthinkable!

The world does not progress with rational analysis, but rather thanks to people who dare to ask "why not?" Success rewards those with a positive mindset, a sense of imagination and risk:

Should we do it?	Why not?
When should we do it?	Why not now?
Who should do it?	Why not me?

The fear of failure and ridicule is a strong inhibitor of the "why not" mindset. Charlie Chaplin used to say, "Failure is unimportant. It takes courage to make a fool of yourself." How many good ideas have never seen the light of day because their inventors were afraid of mockery?

Although the fear for failure is hard to confront, success can be numbing. Many people find it hard to take a different course before a disaster strikes, saying, "Let's wait until we have a problem; then we shall see." Why change a winning horse?

Finally, the "why not" mindset implies focusing on the future. We are all hostages of our history, of habits and of traditions. However, it is sometimes necessary to leave our comfort zones and start over. We should do it when we fail, but also when we sense that a successful model is reaching the end of its lifecycle. The "why not" mindset is also about turning away from the past.

And as John Maynard Keynes rightly said, "The difficulty lies not so much in developing new ideas as escaping from old ones."

Why not?

INDEX OF PERSONS QUOTED

ABOUT THE AUTHOR

Stephane Garelli is a world authority in World Competitiveness, having pioneered this new field of economics. He is Emeritus Professor of World Competitiveness both at IMD business school and the University of Lausanne and the founder of the World Competitiveness Center.

A former managing director of the World Economic Forum and the Davos Annual Meetings, he was also chairman of the board of the FF Sandoz Financial and Banking Holding and a member of the Constitutional Assembly of his local state in Switzerland.

He is currently chairman of the board of the Swiss newspaper *Le Temps* and a member of the International Olympic Commission on Sustainability and Legacy.

He is the author of numerous publications on competitiveness and global business. He is well known for his series of World Competitiveness Yearbooks that highlight and rank the competitiveness of nations. He published his bestselling book *Top Class Competitors: How Nations, Firms, and Individuals Succeed in the New World of Competitiveness* with Wiley.